# GIS *in* Public Policy

Using Geographic Information for More Effective Government

R. W. Greene

ESRI PRESS
REDLANDS, CALIFORNIA

ESRI
    GIS in Public Policy
    ISBN 1-879102-66-8

First printing June 2000. Second printing December 2000. Third printing February 2003.

Printed in the United States of America.

Published by ESRI, 380 New York Street, Redlands, California 92373-8100.

Books from ESRI Press are available to resellers worldwide through Independent Publishers Group (IPG). For information on volume discounts, or to place an order, call IPG at 1-800-888-4741 in the United States, or at 312-337-0747 outside the United States.

# Contents

*Acknowledgments   vii*
*Foreword   xi*
*Introduction   xiii*

**Chapter 1**   **Education   3**
FOCUSING FEDERAL FUNDING   *4*
GIS SOLUTIONS IN IDAHO   *9*
JUGGLING BORDERS AND BOUNDARIES   *16*

**Chapter 2**   **Health and Safety   21**
MAPPING THE WAR ON CRIME   *22*
FIRST STEPS TOWARD HEALTH   *28*
PREPARING FOR THE WORST   *33*

**Chapter 3**   **Public Services   37**
METROPOLITAN GIS   *38*
CUSTOMER ENTRANCE: GIS   *45*
LONE STAR REDISTRICTING   *50*

**Chapter 4**   **Environment   55**
CLEARING THE AIR   *56*
BREAKING THROUGH A BRICK WALL   *62*

**Chapter 5**   **Social Services   71**
MAPPING TRUTHS, MAPPING NEEDS   *72*
OLDER DRIVERS, NEW APPROACH   *80*

**Chapter 6**   **International   85**
YOU CANNOT FIX WHAT YOU CANNOT SEE   *86*
AFTER WAR, MAPPING PEACE   *93*

*Internet Resources   101*

## Acknowledgments

THIS BOOK could not have been written without the help of scores of people at the organizations and agencies profiled, and many others at organizations not profiled but which are no less fervent in their belief in GIS, or skilled in its use. Generosity of time was exceeded only by generosity of patience, and to all, heartfelt thanks:

EDUCATION
Art Serabian and Armen Bacon of the Fresno County Office of Education; Jill Marmolejo of Fresno Unified School District; Talal Albagdadi and Monique Nelson of The Omega Group; Ed Wechsler and Patricia Conner of the Duval County School District; Mike Winston, Charlotte Arnold, Sarah Toy, Michael Johnson, Cathy Sprabeary, and Malissa Hanson of Shelley High School; Linda Cummings of Stuart Elementary School; Paul Muirbrook of Bingham County; and Gene Heaton of dg Associates.

HEALTH AND SAFETY
Tom Casady of the Lincoln Police Department; Carl Walter of the Boston Police Department; Monica Nguyen and Richard Lumb of the Charlotte–Mecklenberg Police Department; Robert Meier of the Overland Park Police Department; Gary Archambault of the State of Connecticut; Garry Lapidus of the Connecticut Childhood Injury Prevention Center; Michael Vachon of Yakima County; Dianne Patterson of Yakima Valley Memorial Hospital; Keith Clarke of the University of California, Santa Barbara; Jay Creutz, Dean Kaul, and John Bruno of Science Applications International Corp.; Paul Bryant of the Federal Emergency Management Agency; Glenn Levy and Claudia Haack–Benedict of the City of Fort Collins; and Liza Casey of the City of Philadelphia.

PUBLIC SERVICES
Mark Epstein, Ginger Juhl, and Kathleen Cain of the Convergent Group; Dave Mockert and Juli Paini of the City of Indianapolis; Stephen Goldsmith and Kim Wilson of Baker & Daniels, Indianapolis; Tim Storey of the National Conference of State Legislatures; Alan Ware and Carol Nemir of the Texas Legislative Council; Anatalio Ubalde of the City of Vallejo; Pablo Monzon of GIS Planning; and Ann Peton of the State of Iowa.

ENVIRONMENT
Paul Penner, Christian Jacqz, Steve McRae, Tim Watkins, and Jeanne Wildman of

the Commonwealth of Massachusetts; Michael Terner of Applied Geographics, Inc.; Robie Hubley of the Massachusetts Audubon Society; Mayor David Cohen of Newton, Massachusetts; David Barenberg of the Oregon League of Cities; Jennifer Kramer and Rona Birnbaum of the Environmental Protection Agency; Bernard Melewski, David Greenwood, John Sheehan, and Joseph Moore of the Adirondack Council; Bob Larson of the National Atmospheric Deposition Program; Larry Sugarbaker and Carrie Wolfe of the Washington Department of Natural Resources.

SOCIAL SERVICES
Anita Bock of the Los Angeles County Department of Children and Family Services; Andrew Dickman and Dwight Danie of the Florida Department of Children and Families; Patrick Burke of Data and Policy Analysis (DAPA) of The Atlanta Project; Patrick McGuigan and Jim Vandermillen of The Providence Plan; G. Thomas Kingsley of the National Neighborhood Indicators Project of The Urban Institute; Katherine Freund of the Independent Transportation Network; Tim Quinn of GeoFields, Inc.; and Steve Thomas of the UCR/California Museum of Photography.

INTERNATIONAL
Azer Kurtovic, Andrej Loncaric, Boran Loncaric, and Jana Belceva of GISDATA; Muhamed Muminovic of AMPHIBIA; Lutfi Kapidzic of the Zavod za planiranje razvoja Kanton Sarajevo; Jay Craig of the Global Network for Rebuilding; Robert Aldridge of Gulf States Paper Corp.;

Kevin Horton of the Camber Corp.; Rifaat Masoud and Jan Ottens of Skylink Aviation; Nate Smith of the Office of Foreign Disaster Assistance of the United States Agency for International Development (OFDA/USIA); David Smith of the State Department; James Jancaitis and Paul Hearn of the United States Geological Survey; Mark Schaefer of the Department of the Interior; and Heather York of Kent State University.

AT ESRI
Gary Amdahl, Eric Bishop, Matt Bottenberg, Dale Brooks, Don Chambers, Andrew Cheney, Carmelle J. Cote, Simon Cottingham, Kevin Daugherty, Bill Davenhall, Marjorie Dougherty, Lisa Fastnaught, Charlie Fitzpatrick, Nancy Forrest, Charles Gaffney, Lisa Godin, Russ Johnson, Tina Kapka, Hugh Keegan, Heather Kennedy, Carole Kolota, Danny Krouk, Richard Lawrence, Eric Laycock, Dana Leipold, Eric Linz, Tim Lux, Merrill Lyew, Scott McNair, Tom Miller, Lew Nelson, Duane Niemeyer, Carl Nylen, Tim Ormsby, Monica Pratt, Mike Ridland, Bob Ruschman, Peter Schreiber, Patrick Showalter, Shelly Sommer, and Christopher Thomas.

Thanks also to Jeanne Rebstock and Christian Harder, who supervised this book's creation; to Michael Hyatt, who designed, produced, and copyedited it with customary precision and elegance, ably assisted by Jennifer Galloway; to Michael Karman, who edited the entire book with flair and vast good humor; to Amaree Israngkura, who designed the cover; and to Terri.

OTHER CREDITS
The photograph from the top of Gothics in Adirondack Park on page 57 is by Gary Randorf and is courtesy of him and the Adirondack Council. The maps of sulphate deposition in 1985 and 1998 on page 59 are courtesy of the National Atmospheric Deposition Program/National Trends Network. The map of the Dayton peace negotiation boundaries on page 96 is courtesy of the Department of Defense.

*Foreword*

WHEN ASKED TO WRITE the foreword to this book, I had just completed six years as the mayor of Fort Collins, Colorado, and had seen first-hand the contribution that GIS made to my community, a contribution it could make to any community, I believe.

Fort Collins is a growing community, and under almost constant scrutiny from its residents about how well that growth is managed. The comprehensive plan that had become effective in the late 1970s, for instance, was already coming under attack by the mid-1980s. The city council knew that we would need a plan that everyone could understand, a plan that communicated through maps. People would need to know not only what changes were proposed, but which neighborhoods would be affected.

The council, the planning commission, a special citizens' group, a consulting group, and the planning staff of the city held more than a hundred meetings and other events. The GIS group would prepare a map for each decision as soon as it was made. During the planning stage, these were used for discussion and further decisions. Usually, revising a comprehensive plan would take several years, but fortunately, Fort Collins had by that time a functioning GIS within the planning department. We were able to complete a new comprehensive plan in a mere 18 months.

The plan continues to be flexible, by design. The first changes to the final plan came about six months after its passage, and it has been updated every six months since then. Thanks to GIS, our pledge to keep the plan current is possible.

Then one night in late July, 1997, disaster struck. After about three hours of steady rain, Spring Creek, ordinarily a quiet, placid stream, became a raging torrent. Just a few weeks before, Fort Collins had received an award and a commendation from the Federal Emergency Management Agency (FEMA) for its storm drainage program and flood insurance rating. How proud I was of that award. Then came the rain. That night, the flood destroyed a mobile home park, a train derailed, and a fire broke out, all in the same area. Colorado State University suffered severe water damage to its buildings and library collections. Our GIS unit already had good maps of the community and of the drainage basins, as well as of all the floodplains. The FEMA officials who came to help needed only one look at our maps to see that they could use them to get us back on our feet.

These experiences show two of the ways that GIS can contribute to public policy. It can help to develop public policies, integrating information from various departments, collected at different times for different purposes, and to communicate those policies to the people affected. What's more, it makes it easy to change those policies to acknowledge changing situations, including unexpected disasters. GIS can not only show where to get help to those who need it most, but can be part of rebuilding after the mess as well.

For many years GIS was known only to a select number of scholars and researchers. Those who trained in natural resources and environmental sciences were among the first to find practical applications for the technology. Now we are poised to see these tools used more and more in formulating the policies that govern our lives.

Developing public policies is often chaotic, filled with the stresses of conflicting values. The more voices heard in the process and the more opinions sought, the more diverse the discussions about what we should do and what solutions to a situation might be. That is what one would expect of a democratic society. GIS can help, not only in presenting the facts but in showing the possible effects of several different solutions. When issues are placed in geographic context, members of the community and policy makers alike can better see the relationships between problems and the solutions proposed. This book offers real cases that illustrate these processes in public policy.

*Ann Azari*
*Fort Collins*

# Introduction

MUCH HAS BEEN WRITTEN about the extraordinary economic effects of the digital revolution: how it has shattered traditional notions of the business cycle, how its hyperefficiencies mean hyperproductivity, how the demand for shinier, faster toys requires a new paradigm of the marketplace.

But not everything that gets done, or needs to get done, in the world is available in the marketplace. The quieter, less celebrated, but no less powerful effects of the digital age are also being felt in public spaces—in city council chambers, in PTA meetings, in state legislature committee rooms, in regional planning commissions.

At the forefront of this expansion into the public sector are geographic information systems, or GIS.

GIS is a powerful software technology that allows a virtually unlimited amount of information to be linked to a geographic location. Coupled to a digital map, GIS allows a user to see regions, counties, neighborhoods, and the people who live in them with unprecedented clarity, showing layer upon layer of information—such as demographic trends, soil types, income levels, voting tendencies, poverty rates, pollution levels, epidemics, cereal brand preferences, high school drop-out rates,

college scholarship rates, television watching preferences, and Internet accessibility—the list is limited only by the imagination. GIS also incorporates powerful tools to analyze the relationships among all these kinds of data. The effects of this new power on public policy are profound.

GIS portrays important information graphically—information that used to be available only as columns of numbers or, at best, colored charts. This simple innovation should not be underestimated. "GIS makes things graphic," says Robie Hubley of the Massachusetts Audubon Society, "which is the way the human brain works, so the connections are so perfectly obvious." Looking at a GIS map of crime rates shows a city council instantly how its public safety funding may need to be shifted; a map of low-weight births shows public health officials how their prenatal-care teen education program is working; a map showing areas where children have been exposed to lead paint gives a school board a clue to low achievement among some students. And these GIS tools are increasingly being made accessible to citizens, policy makers, and the media through the Internet, itself expanding at an exponential rate.

GIS is not new to the world of government and public policy. But like other high-tech phenomena, it has for too long been viewed as the exotic realm of specialists. This is changing. The realization is growing that almost everything that happens in a public policy context also happens in a geographic one: transportation planners, water resources studies, education subcommittees, redistricting boards, planning commissions, and crime task forces all must consider questions of *where* along with the usual ones of *how,* and *why,* and *how much will it cost.* GIS, by answering the first question, helps answer the others.

As the hands of decision makers become more familiar with the tools of GIS, the scope of its capabilities is expanding. Many of the stories here show how GIS is carrying out public policy decisions reached by voters or by their elected representatives. It is doing so with a palpable new efficiency. But others show GIS at the next level, where GIS is becoming an integral part of decision making itself, helping to shape and influence the context in which decisions are made. It is on this level that GIS may have its most profound effects.

Among the enthusiastic supporters of GIS whose voices are found here are decision makers with first-hand experience of its benefits. They include Stephen Goldsmith, former mayor of Indianapolis; Mark Schaefer, former Acting Assistant Secretary of the Interior for Water and Science; Anita Bock, director of the Los Angeles County Department of Children and Family Services; David Cohen, former state representative in Massachusetts and now mayor of Newton, Massachusetts; and Ann Azari, former mayor of Fort Collins, Colorado, and former member of the board of the National League of Cities.

Among the lessons they will tell you they have learned is that for GIS to make a difference for an organization, its power must be recognized by the leadership. "Somebody near the top has to kind of push the organization and understand its importance," says Goldsmith. "It has to be somebody above the day-to-day bureaucracy."

The cases selected here demonstrate the versatility of the technology—how it can serve across the whole range of public policy concerns. They also show the technology's wide use across the entire nation, literally from Maine to California, from Florida to Washington. Moreover, these are typical uses of GIS; while not every user here is pushing the GIS envelope, its benefits are always apparent. Above all, these cases are relevant to areas of policy that Americans tell pollsters matter to them.

The digital age has given new value to that commodity known as information. But those who participate in a democratic system have always known that information is its lifeblood. As an information source, GIS is providing a new and powerful paradigm for governing ourselves.

*R. W. Greene*
*Redlands*

# GIS in Public Policy

"I think by far the most important bill in our whole code is that for the diffusion of knowledge among the people. No other sure foundation can be devised, for the preservation of freedom and happiness. . . . Preach, my dear Sir, a crusade against ignorance; establish & improve the law for educating the common people. Let our countrymen know that the people alone can protect us against these evils, and that the tax which will be paid for this purpose is not more than the thousandth part of what will be paid to kings, priests & nobles who will rise up among us if we leave the people in Ignorance."

Thomas Jefferson, Letter to George Wythe
Paris, August 13, 1786

# Chapter 1

# Education

The increasing use of GIS in education shows how well the technology reaches across diverse fields of human endeavor. While this may surprise those who have stereotyped GIS as the esoteric tool of foresters and hydrologists, the reality is that even in an enterprise as intimate, and crucial, as the education of the young, those who toil there are finding GIS is unquestionably increasing efficiency and adding value.

## Focusing Federal Funding

EVEN BEFORE THE INFAMOUS $317 TOILET SEAT LID, waste and inefficiency in government operations have been easy targets for policy critics and late-night comedians alike. Indeed, it is one area where critics and policy makers can find common ground, for even the most loyal policy defender will concede that implementing policy is a lot harder and less satisfying than conceiving it.

Inefficiencies in American public education have not escaped this kind of scrutiny. In 1995, for example, New Jersey Governor Christine Todd Whitman launched the School Efficiency Program, which fined school districts thousands of dollars if they exceeded what were considered efficient student-to-administrator ratios. The program ran for 16 months before it was retired, opponents and supporters both claiming vindication for their positions. More recently, conservative critics seized on a study by the Organization for Economic Cooperation and Development that they said showed U.S. schools weren't very productive compared to those in other parts of the world.

GIS is helping to blunt such criticism and to streamline school operations in one county in California by making sure federal education funds are fairly distributed among the many schools that need it.

The Fresno County Office of Education is the umbrella administrative agency for 35 independent school districts in California's agriculturally rich Central Valley. Like its counterparts in other counties, the office provides special services to districts, oversees and approves their budgets, and acts as liaison between them and the state Department of Education.

Among its responsibilities is calculating how much supplemental federal money individual schools within the county are entitled to under the provisions of the Improving America's Schools Act (IASA). This Title 1 money, as it used to be called, goes to schools according to the number of low-income children they have enrolled between the ages of 5 and 17. It's the county office's job each year to calculate the number of eligible children in each school so that state education officials can distribute the federal money equitably.

For years, this has been considered an onerous and formidable task. The Fresno office's jurisdiction is a good-sized one. The 35 districts contain 270 individual schools of about 176,000 students. The IASA funds allotted to Fresno County amount to about $37 million. It traditionally took 750 hours of staff time to do the calculations and to prepare the reports that went off to Sacramento. That staff time was squeezed between the months of November and February, a schedule that left very little time to review the final numbers with the individual districts, each of which was keenly interested in those calculations.

A number of inefficiencies confronted Art Serabian, the Fresno office's executive director of information systems and technology, when he began each year's laborious calculations. First, the information he needed was not only on two different systems, it was housed in two different county agencies. His office had data for the schools, while the county's social services agency held the data on the low-income families, who were identified as such if they received Aid to Families with Dependent Children (AFDC). (The AFDC program was replaced by the California Work Opportunity and Responsibility to Kids, or CalWORKS, program, under the Welfare Reform Act of 1996.) The data that the social services agency kept, however, did not show which schools low-income children attended.

A second problem was the quality of the maps of school attendance zones and school district boundaries. They were on paper, even onionskin, some as many as 10 years old. Some were covered in pencil and eraser marks.

The office's basemaps were also on paper and consisted of commercial maps made by the American Automobile Association, or by Thomas Bros. Maps, a well-known California street map maker.

The calculation process would begin when Serabian's office was given the social services agency's nine-track mainframe tapes. They then would match addresses on the tapes to their own records of low-income students from the previous year. In general, they would get matches for about 75 percent—which left almost 14,000 individual records that had to be matched by hand.

"We'd find the address on a paper map—literally, we'd spread them out on the floor," says Serabian. "Then we'd say, 'Okay, that looks like it's over near Fresno (city) Unified,' so we'd grab the Fresno Unified maps, and then we'd say, 'Okay, that looks like it's in the north of Fresno,' so we'd grab the north-of-Fresno school attendance maps." After matching all 14,000 or so addresses, they'd update the database and then send off the report.

After doing it this way for two years, Serabian decided in 1997 that this process could not continue. Not only was it a cumbersome process, it was inaccurate; he thought Fresno County schools, and therefore Fresno County children, were not getting the money and resources the federal government said they were entitled to. "I could not stand another year of doing it the way we were doing it," he says.

Serabian already knew about GIS and had discovered that several other agencies in Fresno County, including the Public Works and County Clerk/Elections departments, were already using ESRI® GIS solutions. In fact, Fresno County had its own small consortium of GIS users who pooled data and collaborated where practical. Serabian wasted no time joining up, and then going to work to revamp the cumbersome, paper-map-on-the-floor method of calculating federal funds distribution.

Working in ArcView® GIS, Serabian first created spatial files, called shapefiles, of individual school districts. This task was simplified somewhat because the Fresno County Clerk/Elections department already owned such files of the school districts' individual governing areas, which it used to conduct school board elections. Serabian merged the trustee areas to create each district map. Once he had that, it was a simple matter to locate each school within the district and draw its attendance zone, using ArcView GIS editing functions. Since most school attendance areas follow streets, the Public Works Department's shapefiles of streets served as a good guide.

With those simple steps, Serabian had eliminated the need for the tattered paper maps the office had been using up until then.

Next, Serabian needed a new digital basemap. He got one by combining a shapefile of streets from the Public Works department and another file of point locations from the County Clerk/Elections department, a file that contained practically every address in the county.

Serabian had his school information; he then needed to join data of CalWORKS

An ArcView GIS display of school districts within Fresno County.

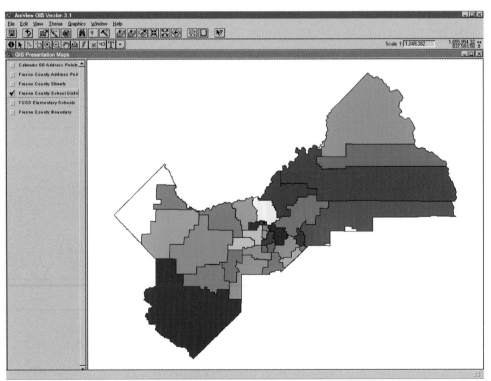

recipients to it. But a digital map of Fresno County CalWORKS recipients did not exist. All that existed were the addresses of recipients, contained in a huge database. Serabian's digital reference map already contained all the addresses in the county. It is a simple matter in ArcView GIS to join a table of data to other tables already associated with a digital map, and this is what Serabian did.

From that point, it was a matter of combining this CalWORKS map with the maps of each district's school attendance zones. Another join operation integrated the CalWORKS recipients' addresses into the appropriate school zone. The process was then repeated for all the schools.

Only a few more steps were needed to assemble this information into reports that were sent to Sacramento.

The Fresno County Office began saving time and money almost immediately.

The entire process now takes 200 hours of staff time instead of 750. The cost of the entire operation dropped more than 70 percent, from $30,000 to $8,000, a savings that easily covered the cost of a powerful new workstation and the

ArcView GIS screen showing Fresno County address points in green and CalWORKS recipients in red. The CalWORKS addresses had existed only in a database, but ArcView GIS easily allows such data to be viewed graphically.

ArcView GIS software. The new digital maps that portray the real state of affairs in Fresno County can be easily updated. And because the process is so much more efficient, county officials now have plenty of time to review their calculations with individual districts, and to make any necessary adjustments.

Late-night comedians and policy critics would find little material to work with in the implementation of Fresno County's education policy. With the help of GIS, it runs more efficiently, and saves money that can be put to use for more important matters—teaching, for example, and learning.

The CalWORKS addresses are now overlaid as points on attendance zone maps of Fresno city elementary schools, showing at a glance which schools have greater need. Individual, confidential records corresponding to the points are available from the database on the left.

## GIS Solutions in Idaho

THE REAL WORLD of Mike Winston's high school students is the smooth Snake River Plain in the southeastern corner of Idaho. To the east at a small distance, the foothills of the Caribou Range rise with a certain authority—the Rockies loom somewhere in the blue-gray sky behind them. To the west, though, it's so flat it might be Nebraska.

On a coldish fall morning, Shelley High School students Cathy Sprabeary, 16, and Malissa Hanson, 17, are crouching in brown grasses along a fence line, next to an irrigation canal, about a half-mile down the road from the school. Nearby, horses twitch in somebody's corral. Cathy sees her stepfather drive by and waves extravagantly. He waves back as he guns his big pickup on by.

Then it's back to the business in hand: studying the tiny screen of a yellow Trimble global positioning system (GPS) unit. The two girls are plotting their exact latitude and longitude, and are working hard at it, checking instruction pages over and over, setting parameters and coordinates, connecting to satellites more than 12,000 miles above. With coaching and help from 21-year-old Sarah Toy, a Shelley High grad working as Winston's assistant, the two girls get the Trimble working the way they want, then march off down the fence line, in search of a Solution.

Mike Winston, science teacher and GIS champion, is the cofounder of the program called just that—Solutions—that embodies his fervent belief that students learn best when they solve problems in the real world of their own communities. GIS is one of the best tools he has found for doing that. So this is no artificial exercise from some tome of education theory that Cathy and Malissa are working on down here under the horses' gaze: along this fence line, spotted knapweed has been seen growing, one of 35 weeds identified officially by the state of Idaho as "noxious," a serious threat to both the environment and the economy. Unchecked, the weeds will damage watersheds, destroy delicate wetlands, and wipe out

R. W. Greene

Cathy Sprabeary, left, and Malissa Hanson figure out their exact latitude and longitude with a GPS unit as part of their Solutions work.

*So many of the kids see no point in learning, but they get interested if the problems are in their own community. I tell them, if you want to help, you've got to be able to do math, you've got to be able to write, and you've got to be able to use a computer.*

**MIKE WINSTON**

rangeland that wildlife need for grazing. Millions of acres have already been lost; the annual national economic loss traced to noxious weeds has been estimated at an astounding $33 billion. An issue rarely, if ever, making it onto a Washington-based network news broadcast, noxious weeds are nonetheless serious business in Idaho and the West.

Once the knapweed location is dialed in on the Trimble, Cathy and Malissa will enter their readings into ArcView GIS software. Dozens of students are doing this mapping, in what is referred to around Winston's classroom-lab as The Weed Project. When completed, the results of the students' weed mapping will be turned over to the Bingham County Weed Superintendent, Paul Muirbrook, who will use those results as part of a base reference map of noxious weed locations in the county. You cannot fight weeds with pesticides or other means without first knowing where they are, or where the problem is most acute, Muirbrook points out. Shorthanded and underfunded as any small public agency in a not-very-wealthy state, Muirbrook is very grateful for the help from the

students. It would take him years to compile the map without their aid, he says.

So the community needs their help, and that makes it an ideal Solutions project for the students of Shelley High, in Winston's view. If students believe in a project, can see that what they do makes a difference, they are more open-minded about learning some skills they will need beyond high school.

"So many of the kids see no point in learning, but they get interested if the problems are in their own community," Winston says. "I tell them, if you want to help, you've got to be able to do math, you've got to be able to write, and you've got to be able to use a computer."

Using ArcView GIS in the Solutions projects requires students to use a similarly diverse set of skills. They need to know some basic operations on the PC just to run the software. They must follow written instructions. They must train their eyes, and hone biology and botany skills, in order to identify different kinds of weeds in the rural greenery. They must learn the intricacies of the GPS, and then use their understanding of math and geography to integrate the GPS results into ArcView GIS. Reports about The Weed Project require grammatical and stylish writing, and public presentations to school boards or other august bodies require public presentation skills.

Not all Solutions projects have incorporated GIS, although they have all incorporated the goal of making the students' world better because they put their skills to work in it. One involved moving a historic but dilapidated one-room schoolhouse into town and renovating it. That required the exercise of skills from the mundane to the sublime—from calculating the cost of roofing materials, to raising money for the move, to recording the memories of octogenarians who attended classes in that schoolhouse long ago.

An early Solutions project that did incorporate GIS helped the Idaho Department of Water Resources by mapping functioning and nonfunctioning wells in the Snake River Plain Aquifer, one of the region's most important natural resources. In another, the school district itself turned to the class for a GIS solution to the problem of drawing new school district trustee boundaries. The class managed to do in about 15 hours what the district had been unable to do over a period of weeks.

Such projects are a lot more interesting—if more rigorous—way of learning these subjects than sitting in a classroom reading out of a textbook.

"It gets kind of complicated sometimes," says Cathy.

R. W. Greene

The genial Winston, here making a point to students in his classroom-lab, is tough when it comes to getting students prepared for life after high school, with skills that GIS helps them learn.

"Yeah, but sometimes I sort of like complicated things," says Malissa.

Similar sentiments come from Sarah Toy, Winston's teaching assistant, on hiatus from college, who helps shepherd the two-person Weed Project teams through their mapping. She has become the resident ArcView GIS expert, without planning to be. The projects she has worked on using GIS have forced her to stretch out intellectually in a variety of ways: learning statistics on one project and brushing up her algebra for another. "I didn't really like math," she says, "and I'm not a visual learner, but ArcView forced me to learn those things." It has also given her considerable experience at teaching, a profession she says she may now pursue.

This secondary benefit—students learning to teach other students—arose from necessity. The teacher who helped start the Solutions program with Winston was also the GIS expert, but he left in 1994. Since Winston didn't know the software that well himself, and since he already had a full workload, he enlisted his daughter Jessica, along with Toy and other students, to be his experts in both using and teaching the software. He scrambled around for grant money to pay them, and says they have become irreplaceable pieces of the Solutions program.

Over the years, Winston and his teaching assistants have assembled a wealth of tutorial material to help students get started with ArcView GIS, including step-by-step instructions, as well as a variety of instructional games. One of these, for example, incorporates geographic knowledge and math to get students mapping the epicenter of an earthquake.

Because ArcView GIS is a powerful program with hundreds of commands and functions, the key is to show students just the basics and then to let them explore further on their own, says Toy. Trying to teach them the entire software program right away only overwhelms them.

Students new to ArcView GIS start by simply going to an atlas in the library and picking out a country. Then, under the tutelage of Toy or Winston's newest recruit, Michael Johnson, they learn how to get ArcView GIS up and running on the PC. They add their country as a theme to an ArcView GIS project, using some of the several megabytes of national and international geographic data that come with the software. They then add cities to the digital map—and learn additional facts about the country. From there, they cruise the World Wide Web to find additional relevant information, such as photos of historic places in the cities. They then learn to use the "hot-link" feature of ArcView GIS, which makes a photograph of the city pop up on the screen when its location on the digital map is selected with the mouse. The students create a simple map layout and print it out; after that, they are encouraged to experiment and get involved in a project.

Compared to adults, teenage students pick up ArcView GIS skills with great ease and speed, says Winston. Kids don't have preconceived notions about what they can and cannot do, or what a computer should and should not do—they are more willing to take chances, Winston figures. Toy's view is that kids also appreciate more quickly the visual way ArcView GIS presents information, and the instantaneous way its map displays can change size, color, or the density of the information in them. Adult teachers often wind up learning the program from students.

Winston delights in this role-reversal. One morning in his busy classroom-lab, he pointed and chuckled. "That's what I love to see," he said. In a corner, a student was tutoring a teacher in basic Microsoft® Windows® and in ArcView GIS, coaching her patiently as she stepped gingerly among Windows directories and file folders. Making maps would come later.

Some of his fellow teachers are coming around slowly to understand how valuable GIS can be in a wide range of subjects, Winston says. One English teacher used ArcView GIS to help map and illustrate Huckleberry Finn's journey down the Mississippi. Winston, who holds a graduate degree in educational administration, says the possibilities for use in other courses, especially non-science ones, are infinite, limited only by the imagination of teachers.

High-school students aren't the only fast learners. At an elementary school down the road from Shelley High, Toy and teacher Linda Cummings are taking third- and fourth-graders through an ArcView GIS mapping project.

Cummings has brought the Solutions theory and practice into her classroom, albeit with a project more their size—they are mapping Shelley's fire hydrants. No map of the hydrants now exists, and the fire department says it could use one.

The class has done field research already, having been driven through town to find hydrants and draw them on paper maps.

At a table, Cummings helps groups of three review what they've done so far. It is clear that these nine- and ten-year-olds fully understand the abstract notion of a map. Cummings helps them transfer hydrants drawn on their own paper sectionals of Shelley to a larger city map, and reminds them of important considerations such as which side of the street a hydrant was on. "We've got to be real accurate so the firemen know exactly where to go, right?" Heads nod.

A few feet away in front of a PC, Sarah Toy is helping another group transfer the information on the paper maps to an ArcView GIS layout of Shelley streets. She helps the group find an appropriate compass rosetta, and then work on labeling streets with the software's graphics tools and drop-down menus. Daniel Cook and Aria Anastasio are particularly adept, quickly figuring out which drop-down menus do what. They accidentally make a label in 48-point type, and giggle wildly at the monstrous result. But there is no hesitation about how to get the label back to proper size, or about what "90 degrees" means when they try to orient the label properly.

Back at the high school, Cathy and Malissa are deciphering the results of their GPS weed readings and transferring them to a quad map of Shelley.

Malissa: "So we were on this side because the canal was over here."

Cathy: "This is the canal?"

Malissa: "This is the river."

A pause.

Malissa: "OK, this is the school, right?"

Cathy: "I'm thinking that the school's over here . . ."

And so on.

Learning how to collaborate like this in order to solve problems is yet another benefit of Solutions. Winston and Toy say that after much experimentation, they have found that teams of two work best. Any more than that, and there tends to be a lot of standing around and not a lot of work.

Sarah Toy, Winston's teaching assistant, helps elementary school students through a lesson in ArcView GIS.

R. W. Greene

Winston is a soft-spoken man who is determined to arm his students with some practical tools for their journeys into the world. In a former life as a Florida building contractor, Winston said he found that a new hire's 4.0 grade-point average was no guarantee he could actually do anything, an experience that gave him a new appreciation for the pragmatic.

"It gave me a whole different view of our responsibilities," he says, by which he does not mean that teachers must emphasize only vocational skills. "Colleges are saying the same thing: they need people who can solve problems, who can work together, who can communicate. It's a no-brainer for us."

Other districts can use the Solutions and ArcView GIS approach, he thinks. Even urban districts that may not have any noxious weeds or aquifers handy still have problems students can solve. They will need a couple of critical ingredients: one is support from school administrators, and the other is money. Winston has the former, and gets the latter by spending much of his limited free time writing grant proposals.

Winston and Shelley High have been helped by a couple of circumstances of economic geography: Idaho is home to the Albertsons grocery store chain, and the chain's well-endowed charitable foundation has been pouring technology money into the state's schools. In addition, just up the road from Shelley is the Idaho National Engineering and Environmental Laboratory, with its considerable federal science resources. Winston also gives much credit to local GIS consultant Gene Heaton of dg Associates, an ESRI Business Partner; Heaton is the local ArcInfo™ expert who has acted as volunteer technical advisor to the Solutions projects for years.

Yet another reason why other schools will find in ArcView GIS a good classroom tool, beyond the fact that it can teach multiple skills, is the fact that GIS is becoming a sought-after technology skill, with some colleges unable to keep up with student demand for GIS courses. Knowledge of GIS software will make his students an even hotter commodity, Winston believes.

And while the GIS community and the GIS market in southeastern Idaho is not large, that circumstance means opportunity, says Winston—a man who seems to see opportunity lurking behind every rock. If there aren't any GIS jobs in the area, he says, then some of his students can learn to create not just ArcView GIS projects of their own, but entire GIS businesses of their own.

Sounds like a Solution.

The Snake River winds through the Idaho landscape near the town of Shelley and near Shelley High, the low, rectangular building on the right.

R. W. Greene

## Juggling Borders and Boundaries

FEW DISCUSSIONS get parents more riled up than the one about changing the boundaries of their neighborhood school. A proposal to move the border between one school and the next usually guarantees a line of perturbed parents ready to speak up, loudly, at the next school board meeting. They may fear their kids will have to walk too far, that friendships will be broken up, that the new school won't be as good as the old one.

But shifting school boundaries is a necessary evil for school districts struggling to keep pace with rising enrollments. Nationally, public high schools are expected to have 29 percent more students in 2009 than they had in 1989, and elementary schools 15 percent more. Managing such increases has become an increasingly complex juggling act for school districts. Additional pressure comes from taxpayers who demand efficient use of their money. A half-empty school building is not an efficient use of space, nor can students contemplate the knowledge of the ages while they are spilling out the classroom doorway.

The Duval County School District in Jacksonville, Florida, whose problems with growth mirror those facing many school districts, has deployed GIS to assist with some of the juggling it must do. The Duval district has more than 125,000 students distributed among 103 elementary schools, 23 middle schools, 19 high schools, and several other specialized schools. For the 1999–2000 school year,

the district used School Planner™, a customized ArcView GIS software product developed and sold by The Omega Group, an ESRI Business Partner, to calculate boundary changes affecting three high schools and eight elementary schools.

One of the biggest headaches administrators face is calculating the countless permutations even a small change can cause. Redrawing one boundary line requires them to consider not merely which students will be affected, but also whether they attend special programs that are available only at certain schools; whether the change could cause a racial imbalance; whether a particular school's special funding could be jeopardized by a loss of students. The effects of a change must be extrapolated out several years, too: will a redrawn elementary school boundary mean empty classrooms at the high school years later? External factors such as local economic conditions, or the prevailing political attitudes toward development, must also be considered.

But because so many of these calculations are geographic processes, they are perfectly suited to a geographic information system such as the School Planner/ArcView GIS software package.

In the old days, the Duval district made attendance boundary changes by hand—and by knee. Ed Wechsler, the Duval district's Director of Pupil Assignment, says that employees had to get down on the floor with a paper map of the city to draw boundary changes right on the map, then calculate laboriously what effects on enrollment each new change might mean. Many districts still do it that way, Wechsler says, with a shudder.

"We can do in five minutes now what literally would take us hours before," Wechsler says. "The clarity of our maps and the related statistical data has represented a quantum leap in our professionalism and ability to respond to district requests."

School Planner is customized for each school district that buys it and includes a voluminous amount of local geographic data, including a digital file of streets, the district's school attendance boundaries, and locations of its schools. The package also incorporates student records on file. These are used to plot home addresses, or other student information, onto the map. Like those of many other districts, Duval's School Planner maps also show potential

hazards for children walking to schools, such as rail lines and bridges.

For the troublesome chore of redrawing attendance zones, School Planner offers to do the entire job from the Boundary Redistricting option on its main menu. Duval's GIS expert, Patricia Conner, chose this option to create boundary change scenarios for the district's 1999–2000 school year.

In each case, Conner first specified the school attendance zone in question, and the students who would be affected. The Redistrict Report button on the School Planner toolbar showed her the number of students living within the current boundary, while excluding those who, for whatever reasons, attend school somewhere else. Then, using the ArcView GIS vertex editing tool, Conner was able to click on a zone boundary line and simply stretch it like a rubber band to encompass a new geographic area, snapping the

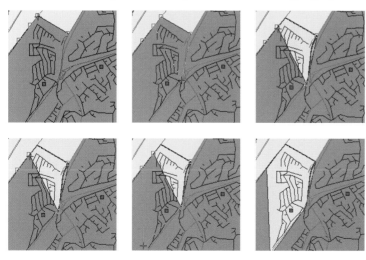

School Planner and ArcView GIS easily allow a school boundary to be changed so that a small subdivision is transferred from the attendance zone at the bottom to the one at the top. In the top row, a corner of the old boundary is pulled down to meet a major road. In the second row, a second corner is pulled down, and the result is that the small subdivision is now a part of the school boundary at the top.

*We can do in five minutes now what literally would take us hours before. The clarity of our maps and the related statistical data has represented a quantum leap in our professionalism and ability to respond to district requests.*

**ED WECHSLER, DIRECTOR OF PUPIL ASSIGNMENT, DUVAL COUNTY SCHOOL DISTRICT**

boundary line into its new place. Once the new boundary was created, Conner could again click the Redistrict Report button to bring up a calculation of how many students had been moved. By merely tugging and pulling on the boundary lines with the mouse, Conner was able to draw and redraw lines, clicking the Redistrict Report button after each change until the desired ratios of students to school were achieved.

Where possible, Conner tried not to break up neighborhoods. She tried also to follow natural breaks in the landscape such as major roads, or natural hazards such as flood-prone streams. The entire process went more smoothly than any other boundary change Conner had done, handling even irregular boundary changes with ease.

For example, in adjusting student ratios between Merrill Road and Parkwood Heights elementary schools, Conner was forced to create a kind of Parkwood

Heights island within the geographic area that belonged to the Merrill Road school. The island contained a new real-estate development. There was no room for the development's students at the overcrowded Merrill Road school, and Merrill Road's own boundary could not be shifted because of a river to the north, a natural, immovable barrier. There was really no alternative to this unusual configuration, Conner said, even though it meant that the district had to start running a bus to pick up Parkwood Heights kids, now somewhat marooned within the Merrill Road attendance zone. In most districts, such odd geographies tend to be the exception, however, not the rule.

As long as people move, and as long as students keep getting promoted to the next grade, attendance zone changes will remain a fact of American educational life. GIS can help make those changes faster, smoother, and easier for everyone involved.

*". . . it is not only the right, but the bounden and solemn duty of a state, to advance the safety, happiness and prosperity of its people, and to provide for its general welfare, by any and every act of legislation, which it may deem to be conductive to these ends. . . ."*

Associate Justice Philip Barbour
The Mayor, Etc., of the City of New York v. Miln
11 Peters 102, 139 (1837)

# Chapter 2

# Health and Safety

Physical well-being is intimately
linked to geographic location. Using
the mapping and spatial analysis
capabilities of GIS, professionals in
the fields of health and public safety
are finding previously undiscovered
links that help them improve the
ways they protect and serve.

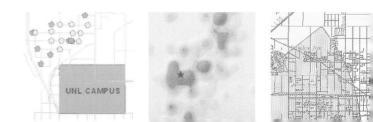

## Mapping the War on Crime

THE BURGLAR liked to add insult to injury.

After he'd stolen the usual stuff—stereo, VCR, jewelry—the burglar liked to indulge in what Lincoln, Nebraska, Police Chief Tom Casady calls "food-based vandalism," dumping the contents of the refrigerator onto the floor—milk, juice, ketchup, whatever—just to make sure you understood your home had been violated.

Lincoln police took notice of him at a monthly meeting of senior officers that Casady held to look at crime statistics and trends and to discuss strategies. To these meetings, he had begun bringing ArcView GIS projects that showed his officers crime patterns occurring in Lincoln. At this meeting, the officers saw two small blobs of burglaries in different parts of the city. Clusters of similar crimes so far apart wouldn't normally get much notice, except that these had all taken place about the same time—and when the officers started discussing them, they discovered all had the peculiar mark of the Food Burglar. That almost certainly meant they were connected. That certainly meant they were worth investigating further.

Lincoln's is one of a growing number of law-enforcement agencies that have added GIS to their crime-fighting arsenals. They are recognizing its value in giving analysts and commanders an instant picture of crime distribution in a neighborhood, a city, a region, or a state. Reports full of words or tables full of numbers might never reveal a crime

pattern that is easily recognizable as such in seconds when it pops up on a GIS display. That display can also show the density of crime, or how crime patterns change across time, or the relationship between crime patterns and other elements in a landscape—bank robbery patterns and freeway on-ramps, for example.

Such patterns are invaluable for understanding where crime is in a city and what resources will need to be marshaled to respond. "Spotting patterns allows you to target your resources a little more tightly, a little less randomly," says Casady. Once police notice such patterns, they can beef up patrols of an area, or check the current whereabouts of those known to have had an affection for a life of crime.

As burglary schemes go, the one that Lincoln police noticed and unraveled with the help of ArcView GIS was small but circuitous. The suspect worked at the circulation department of the city's daily newspaper, and targeted the homes of subscribers who had asked the paper to suspend delivery when they were on vacation. The suspect found house keys in the garages of the vacationers' homes. Police charged that he also burglarized the home of a newspaper executive, and even one of the newspaper's own offices.

While the Lincoln department is not large, with 296 sworn officers and an annual budget of $22 million, it has managed to do much with GIS. Moreover, it does so more or less on a shoestring.

Much of the GIS work is done by Casady himself using ArcView GIS and ArcView Spatial Analyst, with the help of one other employee. Although resources aren't large, Casady says the department is able to do as much as it does by accessing the robust GIS databases that already exist in other city departments, such as public works and streets. That resource is one many other police departments can access, he thinks.

Lincoln and larger departments such as San Diego and Philadelphia may be leading the edge of this new law-enforcement technology, but many others have begun to recognize the potential benefits; the word has started to spread. The federal government's National Institute of Justice has established a Crime Mapping Research Center; at the center's second conference, attendance doubled from the first year's, and Attorney General Janet Reno took note of the growing value of GIS: "Mapping enables us to identify crime-ridden areas to not only direct resources, but ultimately to reduce crime and prevent new crimes from occurring." A 1998 report by the Department of Justice and the National Partnership for Reinventing Government, *Mapping Out Crime*, also lauded the development of GIS as an effective crime-prevention tool. The Justice Department has worked closely with ESRI to develop crime-fighting software. CrimeView®, an ArcView GIS extension specifically designed for law-enforcement applications and sold by ESRI Business Partner The Omega Group, is Omega's best-selling product.

The granddaddy of crime mapping with a GIS is simple pin mapping—sticking pins on a paper map to indicate where crimes are occurring. A GIS, with its limitless databases, allows a considerably greater degree of sophistication and variation on this central idea. The intensity of certain kinds of crimes can be mapped over several months or years to show long-term trends; or they can be mapped against a 24-hour day to show where a second patrol unit might come in handy during lunchtime. Crime incidents can be mapped not just according to a city's boundaries, but also by precinct, showing a commander how better to deploy manpower. Crime maps can show the addresses of people who are on probation or for other reasons required to notify local law enforcement of their whereabouts. And they can show the extent of territory that street gangs claim as theirs.

Crime patterns revealed by GIS can be used to combat problems broader than those posed by one predator. Lincoln police used it to help the University of Nebraska with its student drinking problem, one so acute the school received special grant money to help. Having already beefed up their enforcement of alcohol regulations at college taverns, police saw a subsequent rise in complaints about out-of-control parties and drunk students at private residences in neighborhoods around the school. They mapped those neighborhoods in ArcView GIS and then stepped up their patrols, shutting down parties and arresting students

A GIS map created by Lincoln police showing the decline in complaints about parties near the University of Nebraska–Lincoln campus.

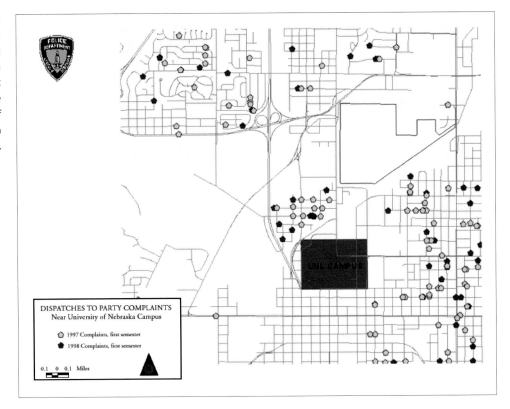

when necessary. The following year, complaints about those out-of-control parties dropped 27 percent.

GIS is also useful in crime prevention. For instance, Lincoln police saw a pattern of automobile break-ins in an area of the city that had lots of apartment complexes. Apartment complexes can be fertile ground for such property crimes, since there is a lot of property concentrated in one area. But that concentration also makes them fertile ground for increasing the public's crime awareness, since it is possible to get the message across to lots of people. In this case, having seen in a GIS the pattern developing around the buildings, a Lincoln officer was dispatched to visit apartment building managers. The officer distributed flyers to be put up in laundry rooms and mailrooms that informed residents of the break-ins, urged caution, and offered crime-prevention tips—such as not leaving CDs and CD cases visible inside cars.

Police departments are also finding that GIS can help solve several crimes at once, or, as the jargon has it, getting "multiple clearances." After officers have arrested someone for committing a crime, they'll confront the suspect with a map showing where other crimes have been committed that have similar characteristics—such as a certain method of breaking into a building, or certain kinds of items stolen. Often, just seeing a geographic pattern that does everything but flash neon signs will cause the suspect to admit to many of those other offenses—sometimes to ones police weren't even aware had been committed.

As law-enforcement use of GIS becomes more widespread, applications beyond crime maps are being developed. For example, some specialists are increasingly interested in an application called geographic profiling that explores the patterns of repeat criminals. An investigative theory emerging from this work is that some repeat criminals won't target victims on or near their own home turf. This may mean that where a series of crimes is *not* occurring could be as important a clue as where they are.

Sometimes it is not officers who need additional information or education, but other agencies or elected officials. Casady recently brought a crime density map he created with the help of ArcView Spatial Analyst to a hearing of the Nebraska Legislature. Legislators were considering funding a new recreation center in Lincoln, and Casady brought the map along to show them how its location made it a good investment. The map illustrated

vividly for legislators the crime densities in Lincoln as they heard Casady argue that putting the recreation center in the middle of a high-crime area would give residents alternative things to do with their time: "These services are important to protecting and stabilizing our most

*I would be hard-pressed to pick which is most significant, the value of GIS for crime analysis and targeting strategies, or the value of GIS for informing the general public. . . .*

**LINCOLN POLICE CHIEF TOM CASADY**

fragile neighborhoods," he told them. "If you want to pick the best spot in the city to improve the physical and social infrastructure, this is it."

Some police departments, including Lincoln's and the Charlotte–Mecklenburg County department in North Carolina, have begun to deploy GIS to work in the newest law enforcement strategy, community policing.

Community policing calls for departments to embrace strategies that increase interaction and communication with the public. This has meant such concrete measures as taking officers out of their tank-like patrol cars and putting them on foot, and setting up small storefront police stations in neighborhoods.

"I would be hard pressed to pick which is most significant," says Casady, "the value of GIS for crime analysis and

A density map of violent crimes in Lincoln that Chief Casady created, using ArcView GIS and ArcView Spatial Analyst, for his testimony before the Nebraska legislature. Such maps can often demonstrate graphically the seriousness of a social problem to a layman better than a chart of numbers could. Here, the star marks the proposed location of a recreation center in the middle of one of the most intense violent-crime areas of the city, as reflected by the intensity of the red at that spot.

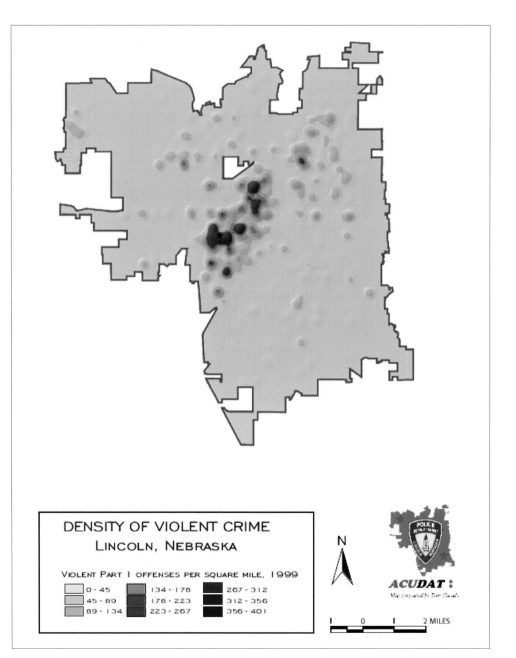

DENSITY OF VIOLENT CRIME
LINCOLN, NEBRASKA

VIOLENT PART I OFFENSES PER SQUARE MILE, 1999

| | | |
|---|---|---|
| 0 - 45 | 134 - 178 | 267 - 312 |
| 45 - 89 | 178 - 223 | 312 - 356 |
| 89 - 134 | 223 - 267 | 356 - 401 |

N

POLICE

ACUDAT :
Map prepared by Tom Casady

0        2 MILES

targeting strategies, or the value of GIS for informing the general public, neighborhood watch groups, neighborhood associations, and individual citizens about the crimes and events in their own neighborhood."

Lincoln has focused its resources in this area on the World Wide Web, where the department uses ESRI's MapObjects® Internet Map Server software to let residents order up their own crime maps from the police Web site. They can also view other data such as lists of recovered stolen merchandise, and of people who have warrants outstanding against them for their arrest.

Casady is pleased with the response to Lincoln's Internet communication effort. The first month the Web site went up, the department recorded 3,900 hits; two months later, the number leapt to 70,000, and more than a year later, it was still holding steady at about 50,000.

"Personally, I think that is where the real power of GIS in policing lies," says Casady, "disseminating valuable, timely, graphical information to citizens and officers."

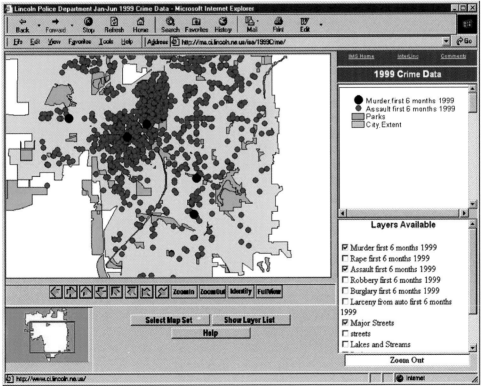

ESRI's Internet Map Server gives Lincoln residents easy Web access to the vast database of crime information in the city's possession, and puts it in geographic perspective. The result for government is a constituency better informed about the location and intensity of problems in the city.

## First Steps Toward Health

THE DEBATE about who is and isn't entitled to various government benefits
and services is a long one, often con-
ducted at a high decibel range. A less au-
dible question, debated among those who
provide such services, is whether those
who are entitled to services in fact receive them—or even know they exist.
With its ability to combine information
with location, GIS is helping public agencies gauge how effectively they are delivering services.

Alarmed at the high rate of infant mortality in Washington State, state legislators created a program in 1989 to increase
the chances that babies born to low-
income or otherwise disadvantaged
women would get a healthy start on life.
The program, called First Steps, gives expectant women extra services beyond the
standard medical and prenatal care they
receive as part of their Medicaid benefits.
These "wraparound" services include pre-
ventive care from public health nurses, di-
eticians and counselors, as well as access to
help for other, nonmedical issues that can
nonetheless affect a child's development,
such as domestic violence.

By the mid-1990s, Washington's infant mortality rate plummeted to one of
the lowest in the nation, and First Steps
was a big part of the reason why.

But in 1998, when the state reviewed
the numbers to see how well the program
was working, health officials in Yakima
County were dismayed to discover that as
many as a quarter of the women eligible

for the First Steps services weren't using
them. This meant more than just a failure
to use taxpayer money optimally. It could
also result in an increase in the number
of underweight babies being born in
the county, each of whom could require
many thousands of public dollars to pay
for intensive neonatal hospital care. In
addition, providers of services, often clinics operating on a shoestring, were missing out on revenue since they weren't
providing services to as many women
as they could be.

The obvious task was to find out where
these women were, why they weren't using the services, and how they could be
persuaded to do so.

That was easier said than done. Yakima
County, located in the south-central part
of the state, is big, at 4,300 square miles,
and has a heterogeneous population of
about 220,000 spread thinly throughout
that space. The poverty rate is high. Gen-
eralizations about Yakima County's population don't work very well because it is so
diverse, says Diane Patterson, director of
maternal health services at Yakima Valley
Memorial Hospital. Finding and survey-
ing women who weren't using services
they were entitled to was a task far beyond the county's abilities. "For us to use
scarce resources to try to blanket this entire county just didn't make sense," Patterson says.

But because of its ability to link large
amounts of data to specific points in space,
using a GIS did make sense. Patterson

and Mike Vachon, director of Yakima County's GIS services, decided to use ArcInfo software combined with data on the county's births to identify areas where services weren't being used fully. They could then identify what kind of women were and weren't using them, and why. Once those questions were answered, the First Step provider organizations could make adjustments to connect better with expectant mothers.

Vachon first obtained the Yakima County birth records from the Washington State Department of Health. He then pinpointed the mothers' addresses, more than 10,000 of them, and marked them on an ArcInfo map of Yakima—a process known as geocoding. From the same records, he identified Medicaid births, which totaled 7,768, or 73 percent—a large proportion by most standards, but commensurate with Yakima's demographics. Vachon then got data from the state Department of Social and Health Services, which kept information about First Step recipients. After converting this data, Vachon also entered those addresses into his ArcInfo digital map. The result was to give him a map of Yakima County that showed thousands of locations—the addresses of women who had given birth in the

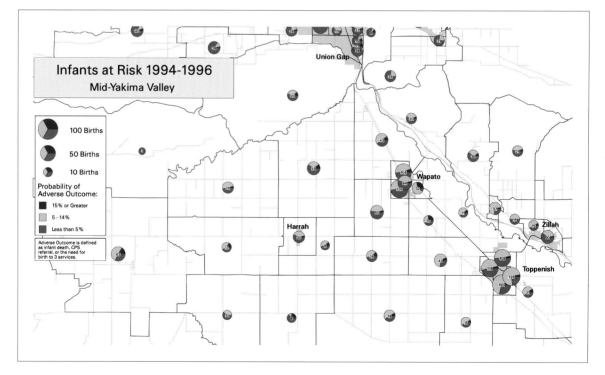

Pie-chart maps showing the distribution, by census block group, of infants in one part of Yakima County who might face serious problems in their early lives for a variety of reasons. The pie-chart map is especially useful because it also shows the intensity of a particular characteristic at a location.

county, and of those, who had and hadn't used First Step services.

Each of the points contained a wealth of information about the mother and each birth, but such information is confidential; Vachon could not simply publish a map of Yakima County's Medicaid recipients. As GIS becomes a more commonly used tool in government, especially in social services, GIS managers are having to resolve this conflict between confidentiality and data that can give researchers valuable information about social problems.

As is often done, Vachon decided to consolidate the information into census block groups, which contain about 250 to 550 addresses—an area large enough to

remove the identification of an individual address, but small enough to connect a trend with an identifiable area. He then created maps of all the births in the county, showing the age and education of the mothers, and where they were born; the chances that a baby would have problems of any kind after birth; and whether or not its birth was paid for by Medicaid.

Vachon says these pie-chart maps were particularly helpful when he and Patterson visited legislators for discussions of health-care funding priorities, because they could tell at a glance how serious a problem their area might have.

The maps helped at least one social service organization shift gears. A Vachon-

Another example of the pie-chart or multivariable display of a different part of Yakima County, which shows at a glance the proportions of the ages of mothers at a location, as well as the total number of births.

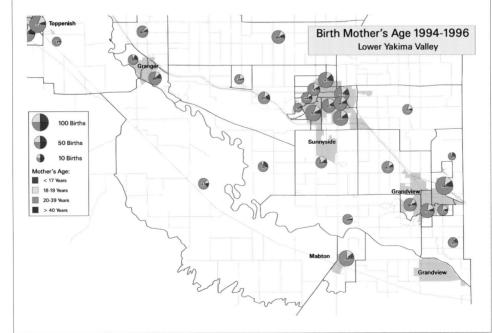

created map of teen pregnancies showed the managers of Project Change, a program in which teenagers counsel other teens on sexual matters, that they needed to strengthen their program in some areas.

But Vachon still needed to pinpoint with more accuracy than broad census block groups where the First Steps message wasn't getting through. The block groups were particularly unsuited for viewing Yakima County's characteristics because some of them took in large chunks of uninhabited land. On a thematic map, these would tend to exaggerate a trend. He also wanted to give overworked providers a simpler map by which to judge the program's success. And

because he was working with relatively small numbers of births, he needed a way to average those numbers so they could be interpreted accurately.

Combining work done by geographers Gerard Rushton of the University of Iowa and Stan Openshaw of the University of Leeds, Vachon developed a spatial filter, using ESRI's ARC Macro Language (AML™). He placed his original maps of geocoded births onto a grid of cells one-quarter-mile wide. His program then ran the filter over every grid cell on the map. As it passed over each cell, the filter calculated the number of Medicaid births, as well as the numbers of births that did and did not use First Steps services. It

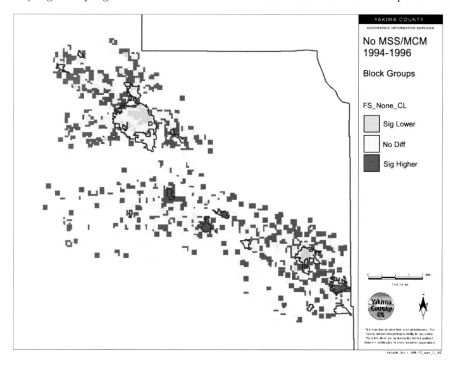

The map that resulted from the spatial filter processing of First Steps data, showing in a simplified way where First Steps services, called Maternity Support Services (MSS) and Maternity Case Management (MCM), were being used more or less than the county average.

then calculated an average for each cell based on the cells around it. It did this for every cell on the grid, a program that required eight to ten hours to run even on a fast computer.

When it was done, however, Vachon's program had produced a map that could be understood in a second, showing small blocks of First Steps usage, colored according to whether the block's usage was above, below, or no different from the county average.

His work told First Steps providers that their services were not getting used as much as they could in three areas, the cities of Toppenish, Grandview, and Wapato. It also showed them that in some places where they didn't expect it their services were being used at a better-than-average rate, for instance on the city of Yakima's low-income east side. Vachon says credit for that went to neighborhood clinics that had been around for a long time and had built up a reputation and relationship with east-side residents.

The analysis also showed that in large part, those women specifically targeted for First Steps services—younger, less educated women who were not born in the United States—were in fact receiving the services at an acceptable rate. It was the women not in that group—that is, older women, American-born, with a better level of education—who were being underserved, and therefore a group that providers needed to target better.

Patterson says that one important benefit of the maps was in validating what was already known anecdotally. Home-visiting nurses probably could have drawn the maps independently just because they knew the territory so well, Patterson says. But the maps, created with a GIS and with accepted statistical tools, reinforced what was already known to be true.

Washington's policy makers decided they wanted the state to be a healthier place for babies to grow up in and thrive, and with the First Steps program, they succeeded in making that a reality. Deploying GIS in Yakima has helped assure that success will be shared by an even greater number of their constituents.

## Preparing for the Worst

IN THE 1990S, there were so many images of disaster they would have numbed the mind if they weren't already tearing at the heart: men, women, and children picking through the charred skeleton of a home, or dangling from helicopters above raging floodwaters, or lying on cots in high-school gyms. It was the worst decade ever in the United States for natural disasters: hurricanes Andrew, Fran, Georges, Iniki, and Floyd; wildfires in the West; 100-year-floods in the Midwest; the Northridge and Landers earthquakes; El Niño storms; paralyzing blizzards in the Northeast.

And in the middle of this decade of destruction came a new horror, a distinctly unnatural disaster in Oklahoma City that destroyed 168 human beings and many more lives beyond those. Acts of terrorism like this were supposed to happen only in distant lands, it was naively thought.

But from these ashes rose a new determination among policy makers to find better ways to prepare for the next disaster. Congress passed, and President Clinton signed, new legislation intended to reduce terrorism on U.S. soil. And the organization detailed to help Americans dig out from disasters, the Federal Emergency Management Agency (FEMA), announced it was switching from defense to offense, and would begin to focus on disaster readiness rather than disaster recovery.

FEMA had developed a powerful new tool with which to make that shift, one usable by emergency services managers from the federal to local level. Known as the Consequences Assessment Tool Set (CATS), this GIS software package is a Swiss army knife of disaster management, made up of several specialized integrated software modules, easily installed on a laptop.

CATS was itself born out of disaster.

Right before Hurricane Andrew hit Florida in 1992, FEMA employee Paul Bryant modified FEMA's computer models of nuclear destruction to estimate the potential damage Andrew might bring; he figured that as many as 260,000 people might need FEMA's disaster-relief services by the time Andrew was through with its rampage. His superiors used conventional damage estimate methods, however, and prepared to help about 20,000 people.

That decision cost the agency dearly. Their 20,000 estimate was grossly short of the actual 310,000. FEMA was caught completely unprepared, unable to help thousands of Florida residents who had lost everything. Newspaper columns were filled with tales of frustration, and some in Congress talked of getting rid of the agency altogether. In the post-mortem, inspectors and auditors recommended that the agency pursue further Bryant's idea of modifying nuclear disaster computer models.

The result was the CATS software package, which the Science Applications International Corp. (SAIC), an ESRI

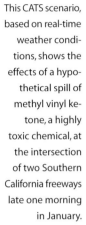

This CATS scenario, based on real-time weather conditions, shows the effects of a hypothetical spill of methyl vinyl ketone, a highly toxic chemical, at the intersection of two Southern California freeways late one morning in January.

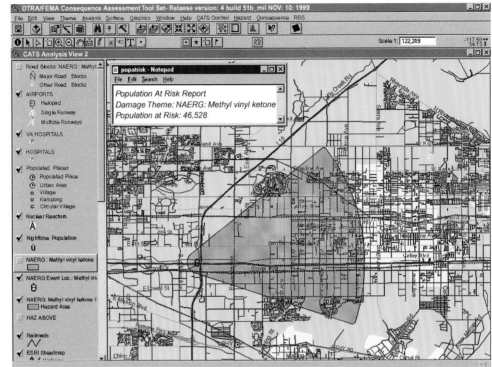

Business Partner, developed with FEMA and the Defense Special Weapons Agency.

CATS is also used to prepare for other natural disasters such as earthquakes; for industrial accidents such as marine oil spills or toxic chemical derailments; for terrorist acts such as bombings and chemical and biological attacks. Among its more chilling capabilities is one that estimates the number of human deaths and injuries to be expected from these nightmares.

A full CATS installation includes ArcView GIS, the ArcView Spatial Analyst and ArcView StreetMap™ extensions, and the disaster modeling software. Despite

the complex analysis the program is capable of, its interface looks only slightly different from the standard ArcView GIS interface. The installation accesses a huge amount of data when modeling disaster scenarios. Besides the complete StreetMap database of U.S. streets, it includes all airports, hospitals, railroad bridges, dams, cemeteries, power plants, refineries, and nuclear power plants in the United States.

CATS can not only predict the path of a hurricane, but also shows the areas outside it that will suffer storm surges and flooding. Its scenarios can be further refined on the spot by downloading information on current conditions from the National Hurricane Center, the National Weather Service, or the United States Geological Survey. It can show where particularly vulnerable populations may be living, such as nursing home residents or jail inmates, whose mobility is restricted.

CATS helps with recovery, too, not only by predicting casualties, but also by estimating the type and amount of recovery supplies that will be needed. It can use satellite imagery to show disaster managers the extent of emergency conditions.

Federal officials have used CATS to prepare for potential terrorist actions at a variety of high-profile public events, including the 1996 Atlanta Olympics and the G8 summit in Denver in 1997.

CATS began showing its utility and its accuracy quickly. Before Hurricane Emily in 1993, FEMA used CATS to estimate that 674 homes would be damaged; the actual number was 683. They were similarly on the mark with the 1994 Northridge earthquake, estimating they would get about 560,000 applications for help; they got about 570,000 legitimate claims. The next year brought Hurricane Marilyn to the Virgin Islands. The agency got about 5,300 applications for help; CATS estimated they would get about 5,100.

There is little people can do about natural disasters, except respond to them as best they can. GIS is helping make that best response a little better.

*"We can no longer afford to pay more for—and get less from— our government. The answer for every problem cannot always be another program or more money. It is time to radically change the way the government operates—to shift from top-down bureaucracy to entrepreneurial government that empowers citizens and communities to change our country from the bottom up."*

Preface, *Report of the National Performance Review*, September 7, 1993

*Chapter 3*

# Public Services

The efficiencies the digital age has brought to private enterprise have helped raise the bar for productivity and service. Voters have begun to expect similar efficiencies from public enterprise as well. With their responsibility for serving the public organized by geography, public agencies are finding in GIS a wealth of tools with which to realize these efficiencies.

## Metropolitan GIS

DIRECTING VOTERS to polling places, routing snowplows through blizzards, tracking potholes and street closures, issuing permits, repairing roads—myriad, common responsibilities of city government, and all getting done in one American city with uncommon efficiency.

GIS serves the city/county government of Indianapolis and surrounding Marion County with exceptional thoroughness. GIS has proven itself to be an essential municipal tool, one that's not just for a handful of specialists building exotic, one-shot applications, as often happens in organizations. Rather, GIS in Indianapolis is helping more than five hundred government employees do the ordinary, everyday tasks of local government more easily and efficiently. Those few sectors of this municipal enterprise that haven't been touched by GIS won't stay isolated for long, for its planners envision more than a thousand employees eventually using a customized version of ArcView GIS on a daily basis. They envision also an expanded Web site that will incorporate this system-wide GIS, so that more city residents can do at home tasks they used to have to go to city hall to do—saving the city money and themselves time.

The city/county government of Indianapolis and Marion County boasts one of the most extensive enterprisewide local government geographic information systems in the nation, in use by more than five hundred employees in all areas of municipal service.

Indianapolis' broad commitment to technology—and especially to technology that gives citizens better access to government services—originated with a firm push from the top in the early 1990s, a time when technology in local government was known and used mostly by a small, isolated group. Then a new mayor came along.

"We needed to move to a higher level of customer service, and we needed to re-think the way we delivered our government products," explains Stephen Goldsmith, mayor from 1992 to 2000, and a close advisor to George W. Bush. "We needed technology for communications and technology for reengineering, and I thought a GIS-based system would be a common denominator of those."

Easier access to the raw materials of decision making, through GIS and the Internet, has been the result.

Take land use, for example, typically enshrined in a city's Comprehensive Plan or similarly named document. At one time, and in many cities still, examining the plan would mean trekking down to city hall through snow-covered streets on a lunch hour. Once there, you might be directed to a dusty basement office to paw through rolls of oversize maps that require three hands to unfurl.

In Indianapolis, the Comprehensive Plan is already available on the city/county's voluminous Web site known as IndyGov. Installed on IndyGov is ESRI's MapObjects Internet Map Server (IMS) application, allowing anyone with a modem to select the comprehensive plan

from a fistful of data layers and bring up the same maps found in the dusty basement office.

Ease of access is only half the benefit that GIS capability brings to IndyGov. The application allows for something you couldn't do with the paper maps—mixing and matching different data layers, allowing new ways of looking at the city: sewer maps can be combined with a map of streams and water resources, demographic maps with ZIP Codes.

Still, the time often comes when every citizen may have to trek to city hall through the snow. Here, too, Indianapolis has put GIS to work at a more mundane, but quintessentially municipal, task.

Historically, Indianapolis hasn't gotten much snow in a typical winter, but all agree that those occasions when it did were noteworthy—for the inefficiency with which the city got rid of it, or didn't get rid of it. City crews went out to plow or salt roads in such haphazard fashion that some roads got cleared four times, while others got cleared not at all. The private subcontractors who were frequently called in to help instead caused more difficulties. Too enthusiastic at their work, they would light up the city's switchboard with complaints from citizens about ravaged lawns and decapitated mailboxes.

This brand of inefficiency was not only expensive, it was embarrassing: when a manager would call in the middle of a snowstorm to find out just how deep a dent a particular storm was putting in the city's treasury, nobody was able to

Indianapolis' Comprehensive Plan, which shows designated land uses throughout the city, is served by ESRI's Internet Map Server application, and is easily accessible on the Web with a browser. The user can easily view other data layers by scrolling the list in the lower-right frame and checking the appropriate box, combining layers when necessary for a more focused analysis.

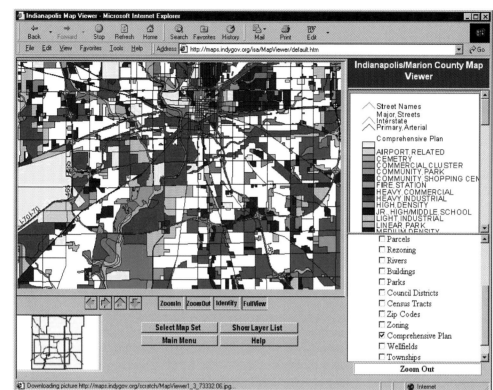

say for sure. It could take weeks to account for all the extra gas, the salt and calcium spread on the roads, the regular and overtime wages, and other associated costs. Slowness was not the worst of it. There was no way, for example, to pinpoint which of the overenthusiastic subcontractors had chewed up a lawn or taken out a mailbox, so the city would be forced simply to write checks from the public treasury to whoever complained.

This haphazard method of removing snow was hardly an advertisement for municipal success.

A new application has transformed all that. Indianapolis, with the help of GIS consultant and ESRI Business Partner Convergent Group, has put together a customized application called Snow Fighter. It combines MapObjects Internet Map Server, an Oracle® database, and other software into one package that has now made cleaning up after snowstorms a concerted exercise in efficiency.

Managers in charge of keeping Indianapolis in business during a snowstorm use Snow Fighter at a centralized dispatch room where they monitor displays showing them which roads need to be cleared first and how quickly, which crews are falling behind and may need help, and the overall pace of the cleanup. Snow Fighter assigns crews and equipment and tracks them, eliminating duplication; tracks the inventory of salt and calcium the city has on hand and how quickly it is being depleted; and tracks expenses. Snow Fighter also keeps an eye on the streets being cleared by subcontractors, so that if any dead-mailbox calls come in, the city knows exactly who to bill for reimbursement. Reports about the costs of a particular operation can be generated right away. Dave Mockert, the city's GIS manager, says that Snow Fighter, during the first snowstorm in which it was used, generated a report of 15 days' worth of snow clearance in a half-hour. Even that was too long for Mockert, who says he will soon be getting reports within minutes.

Cities have to contend not only with the forces of nature but also the forces of the federal government.

The federal Americans with Disabilities Act requires that cities account for all the sidewalk curb cuts within their jurisdictions, to ensure that they meet ADA handicapped-access requirements. In Indianapolis, that meant roughly sixty thousand intersections had to be inventoried. The city assigned one worker to the job, who went out every day with a tape recorder, visiting each curb cut location and examining it, recording its location and condition and any other relevant factors. Then he would go back

to the office, transfer the notes onto a paper form, and ship it off to the data-entry folks.

The result after three years was twenty thousand records, says Mockert, and a good possibility the city would have to hire additional workers to meet the federal deadline. Moreover, because of the circuitous data-entry method, some questioned the accuracy of the inventory up to that point.

Mockert's department built a custom application from ArcView GIS called the ADA Ramp Extension, and installed it on the inspector's laptop. Using drop-down menus and a database of locations, the inspector can now work far more quickly. Creating the extension took about a third of the labor it would take to check and correct all the records entered on paper. The city was no longer looking at hiring additional workers and is confident of fulfilling the ADA requirements.

Other customized applications the city has developed streamline the work of many. One such application keeps track of street repairs. To minimize the number of times a street is torn up and a neighborhood disrupted because of underground work, this application helps crews from different agencies and utilities coordinate their schedules, so a street need be torn up only once. Another application tracks pothole repairs through the city information system, from the time the first complaint is filed until the pothole is filled in.

Another customized application more closely adheres to the city's longer-range strategy of incorporating GIS so as to bring efficiencies and other benefits across the entire enterprise.

That is the Data Viewer, customized for accessing Indianapolis' GIS data and allowing employees to access its power with a minimum of training. Data Viewer comes in two versions, a basic and an advanced, each of which lets the user merely check off the appropriate data layers needed, and then access a map wizard to make presentations, or for other purposes.

The five-hundred-plus users of the Data Viewer are spread across the city in more than a half-dozen different departments.

They include employees in the parks and recreation department, assessors, planners, and city council members.

If data is the frame on which a GIS house is built, then Indianapolis has constructed a mansion. There are more than 160 layers of data for its employees to choose from, and more being added all the time. The variety of these is enormous: fiber-optic conduits, drainage ditches, historical districts, interstate highways, hydrants, manholes, and street-sweeping routes, to mention only a few.

Construction of this structure began in the mid-1980s, very early days for GIS, when a consortium of utilities and city

The Data Viewer application lets city employees choose from scores of different maps of the city, from cemeteries and congressional districts to building and aerial photos. Because the city customized ArcView GIS to create the Data Viewer, employees can access GIS power in a short time, with minimal training.

and county departments agreed to pool resources—and $8 million—to develop a 320,000-parcel, 500-square-mile digital basemap, housed at Indiana University, and called IMAGIS (Indianapolis Mapping and Geographic Infrastructure System). One of the first such partnerships in the country, the idea was that each of the participating organizations could take the common data on the basemap and build their own GIS systems on top of it. Each individual agency's GIS would be stronger because of the breadth and depth of the data supplied by all.

Some created robust systems and put GIS to work quickly. Others did not. Indianapolis' system languished for several years.

Then Mayor Goldsmith was elected and began reinventing Indianapolis government before that phrase became fashionable. He and his staff scrutinized municipal services to see which were useful and efficient. They took some services away from government entirely and gave them to private business—not the most popular policy—and looked for ways to improve those that were left.

"I went down and had the folks doing the existing GIS work show me their stuff," says Goldsmith, "which was really impressive but totally underutilized."

A few GIS specialists handled any and all requests for maps or other GIS-related material, a situation that pleased neither those who needed the maps, nor the GIS specialists who had to do all the work. Moreover, several million dollars had been spent with very little to show for it.

"It was a terrific tool—for about three people," says Goldsmith.

Determined to increase the size of that group, the city awarded a six-year, $18 million contract to the Convergent Group, a Colorado-based IT consulting firm that had helped develop IMAGIS in the 1980s. The mandate to both Convergent and the city's GIS team was to transform the city's large, unused investment in data into some GIS applications that would be of immediate, visible value, and to spread GIS far and wide across the city enterprise. Applications such as Snow Fighter and the Data Viewer are beginning to fulfill that directive.

Goldsmith says one of the biggest obstacles to overcome in order to make the whole system work was resistance to change.

"There's a number of things that people say can't be fixed which always can," he says. "'These two systems can't communicate' generally means that they can, but it's just too much trouble to think about."

GIS efforts in the city are closely managed, through an executive steering committee, through annual strategic planning sessions, and through quarterly reports to a committee of the city council. Among their mandates: develop more applications to let Indianapolis residents access more services through GIS and through the IndyGov Web site. One of these on the drawing board will let residents apply for and receive permits of any kind electronically, without a single trip to city hall. Another will let them map out bus routes from their home to wherever they want to go. Yet another will let them visit the park department's IndyGov Web page and make reservations for family parties or tennis court time.

In short, the mandate is to continue bringing uncommon efficiency to the myriad, common activities of city life.

## Customer Entrance: GIS

IN ONE WAY, the California city of Vallejo differs from most American cities: its location in that ring of urbanity known as The Bay Area. Among the many benefits of standing in the shadow of one of America's most glamorous destinations is that Vallejo commuters can take ferries to work as well as freeways, then hop on cable cars to get to the office.

In another way, however, Vallejo differs not at all from many other American cities: the end of the Cold War brought an end to one of its economic mainstays, a military base.

In Vallejo's case, it was the Mare Island Naval Shipyard, which shut down in 1996 after more than a hundred years of building and repairing all manner of naval vessels. It was the Navy's oldest facility on the West Coast, and an essential element of the considerable military–industrial infrastructure of the San Francisco–Oakland metropolitan area. The official estimate of total jobs lost when the base closed was just under ten thousand.

Every city needs economic development, but in those that lost bases, such as Vallejo, that need becomes acute.

A big part of economic development is simple salesmanship—showing off your city, making sure that the benefits of setting up shop in your neck of the woods, rather than someone else's, are quite obvious.

And Vallejo at the time of the closure had some very real benefits to show off.

Not being San Francisco meant that rents were not beyond all reason. Vallejo straddles an interstate transportation corridor linking Silicon Valley and the Bay Area to points east. Its waterfront real estate on San Pablo Bay was another advantage.

But in the Economic Development department of the city, making Vallejo visible was consuming huge chunks of staff time. And it was, for all the effort, still an inefficient process.

Typically, department employees such as Anatalio Ubalde, economic development analyst, would get calls from developers and out-of-town businesses wanting to know intimate details of the local real estate: whether the city had any industrial space available of at least 50,000 square feet, with railroad access; or whether any developers had retail locations of 2,500 square feet for rent that were also near a mall. Questions about Vallejo's market also figured prominently: did consumers in a certain section of town have much extra cash lying around to spend in a new store? Were education levels of prospective employees high enough?

Such questions added up to a lot of information to compile from many sources, and not enough staff or money to compile it. If the property sought was too small, the city didn't even have a record of it. If it did have a record, it might take a day to track down all the particulars, and then another day or so of phone tag and voice mail to get the information to the person who wanted it.

It was hardly an award-winning way to convince people with money and jobs that Vallejo was the place to bring them to.

But less than two years later, using GIS, Vallejo's Economic Development Department had in fact won numerous national awards for the depth and efficiency of its economic development services. Cities from around the country were on the phone asking how they could do what Vallejo has done.

What Vallejo did was simultaneously increase its visibility and reduce its own workload using GIS. It put its real-estate wares up on the Web, and gave over responsibility for updating the information to those who knew that information the best, the real-estate community itself. The result is a low-maintenance, highly interactive, GIS-based Web site considered one of the most innovative in the nation, and a model for other cities. The site is the epitome of salesmanship, answering questions about industrial space near railroad tracks, or retail space for rent near malls, with stupefying specificity.

It is as up-to-date as the real-estate community wants it to be, because they are the ones who maintain the data.

The Vallejo Economic Development Information System (VEDIS) had its beginnings when Ubalde and the department began casting about for an alternative to the phone-tag-voice-mail-wait-two-days way of doing business. Ubalde knew that what potential investors

wanted from an economic development department was an accessible, up-to-date inventory of its available properties, as well as information about consumers. Since this kind of information was both geographic and suitable for storage in a database, GIS was an obvious solution to Ubalde. He had learned about the technology's potential from his days as an urban planning graduate student at the University of California, Berkeley. The city also needed a way to get this information out to a lot of people at once, and to do so cheaply; the Internet, mushrooming into public consciousness, seemed an equally obvious solution.

The winning bid to invent this system went to GIS Planning, Inc., an ESRI Business Partner that had previously done real-estate GIS work for a nonprofit foundation in San Francisco. GIS Planning founder Pablo Monzon also had a background in urban planning.

The local real-estate community needed little convincing to come on board, Ubalde says, because the potential efficiencies were so obvious. The enthusiastic response, coupled with a favorable story in the *Wall Street Journal,* spurred the city into going online earlier than planned.

Those efficiencies begin in the Map Room of the site, accessible from a link on the opening screen. The visitor sees a map of the city, delivered by ESRI's ArcView Internet Map Server (IMS), customized by GIS Planning. The city considered several GIS/Internet software solutions, but settled on GIS Planning's

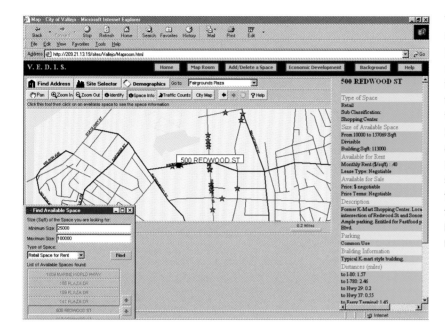

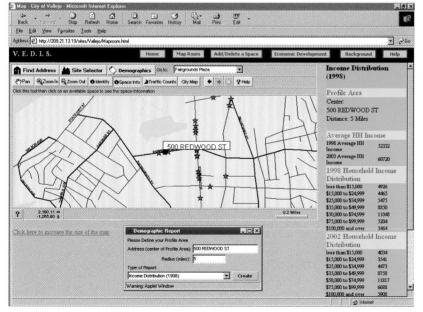

The top screen of the VEDIS application, powered by ESRI's ArcView Internet Map Server technology, shows the results of a query for information on rental properties between 25,000 and 100,000 square feet. The building at 500 Redwood Street fits the bill; additional details are shown to the right on the display. The second screen, below, shows the results of a request for further information about the potential buying habits of the population within a 5-mile radius of the Redwood Street location.

choice of the ESRI product because it was simple and self-contained, Ubalde says. One of the rejected solutions, for example, required users to install a plug-in on their own PCs.

From this overview map, a visitor intent on finding a specific kind of real estate need only click on another button. That brings up a dialog box in which the visitor enters space requirements. The city's server processes the request and presents a list of sites that fit the bill.

IMS can then zoom in on the map to each of the addresses it has found and provide details about the site, such as the availability of parking or the accessibility to highways. In many cases, a photo of the property is also served up.

Clicking yet another button lets the visitor see a variety of demographic data relevant to the site—the amount of money that people living nearby make, or the amount of money that they spend.

Local real-estate brokers help make VEDIS more than just another pretty city Web site. They supply the information about which of their properties are available and for how much.

When the brokers sign up to participate, they are given a user name and

A query about one of the buildings on Mare Island, a former military shipyard whose closure gave new impetus to Vallejo's economic development efforts, gives the user an aerial view as well as essential information about the building. Having all this information available on the Web frees up city employee time and labor.

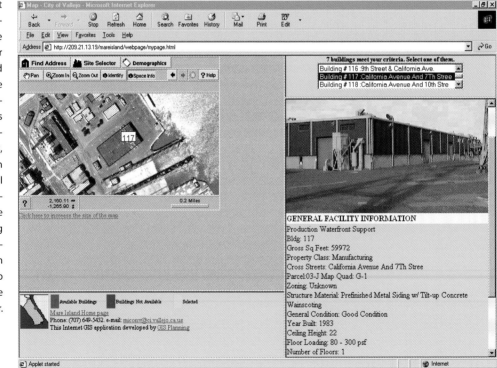

password that allows them to enter information in the database and to add and subtract properties as they are sold or become available. The site stays up-to-date because the real-estate community keeps it that way.

"It's a partnership," says Ubalde. "We market their properties for free and they are able to do deals that bring new jobs and taxes into the community."

Another part of the Web site leads visitors to a map of the former Mare Island base, and allows visitors to search for suitable real-estate space, much of it property left by the Navy. While some of these buildings are so old they will probably be torn down, others could still be useful for manufacturing and other purposes.

Other portions of the site are devoted to less graphically oriented, but still important, details about the advantages of settling in Vallejo, such as the various tax and other incentives the city is willing to give to eligible businesses.

The application was put together originally for only about $40,000, says

*It's a partnership; we market their properties for free and they are able to do deals that bring new jobs and taxes into the community.*

**ANATALIO UBALDE, ECONOMIC DEVELOPMENT ANALYST, CITY OF VALLEJO**

Ubalde, including the data. Unlike many cities, Vallejo did not have a fat property or street or public works database on which to build the GIS; it had to buy one from a commercial vendor. The database layers the city will develop later will be used to give the site an even richer information vein for developers and investors to mine.

However Vallejo may or may not resemble other cities, its economic development innovations have made it stand out. Ubalde notes that the Vallejo solution, a GIS, was not one the city had to stretch to get to—GIS simply provided the shortest distance for the city to get where it wanted to go.

## Lone Star Redistricting

THE NATURE OF THEIR WORK makes legislators both generalists and specialists. They naturally have particular interests and knowledge in health care, perhaps, or water rights, or crime and punishment, but they must also make decisions on the entire panoply of public policy issues.

One issue in which they all specialize, however, is redistricting.

The periodic redrawing of the lines of legislative districts, and the reapportionment of population among those districts—known collectively as redistricting—is mandated by state and federal constitutions and is a task taken most seriously by every legislator. Among other reasons, it is a supremely important job politically. If the lines of a legislative district can be drawn so that its population is homogeneous, either politically or demographically, that can guarantee a political party or a legislator a safe seat for years. The more such seats, the more certain will be the success of a party's legislative and political agenda.

For all these reasons, redistricting clashes are some of the most hard fought of all on the legislative battlefield, so much so that it is not unusual that judges or appellate courts wind up drawing the maps themselves. Given the difficulties that most redistricting plans run into—political feuds and lawsuits, most commonly—court-drawn maps are not an entirely unexpected result.

A new round of redistricting will begin in 2001 when population figures are available from the 2000 census. Legislators will be required to satisfy not only political and arithmetical imperatives, but also provisions of the federal Voting Rights Act, which forbids drawing district boundaries that discriminate against ethnic and linguistic minorities. Recent Supreme Court interpretations of the act have further complicated its application.

Redistricting issues are sheer geography issues. And as GIS has become the technological tool of choice for any question of geography, redistricting is no exception. With the considerations confronting legislators so numerous, GIS will also be an indispensable tool for most states in 2001. One of the most advanced redistricting applications is in Texas.

The GIS programmers and analysts in the Texas Legislative Council, which is responsible for the nuts and bolts of redistricting, are customizing ESRI software to create Texas-specific applications. These will let state senate and house members create and modify new district maps themselves on PCs in their offices. It will allow the effects of even small changes to be seen instantly, bringing up a report of the number of citizens affected by the change. A second customized application, using ESRI's MapObjects Internet Map Server (IMS), will let the public view on the Internet redistricting proposals submitted for consideration; it will also let legislators view those proposals on their laptops on the floor of each house, while debate is going on.

While in some places redistricting is done by a small group behind closed doors, that is not the case in Texas, where accessibility is a priority. So is speed, and that will be a welcome change. In the days before GIS, new maps and redistricting proposals were an exercise in slowness, with each new proposal having to be laboriously transferred to paper maps and then distributed to 181 members.

Speed will be an even more prized commodity for the Texas legislature in 2001, because the peculiarities of both federal and state statutes mean it will have only 57 days to draw up new state senate and house maps.

The redistricting application the Legislative Council has designed for legislators, called RedAppl, is built on MapObjects and Microsoft Visual Basic® technology and has a standard Windows interface. It is intended to be so intuitive it will require no technical support, so that legislators can work on plans into the early morning hours without assistance. It will require only a minimal amount of special training.

A legislator will choose from the interface which jurisdiction to work in, then zoom to that area—whether a thinly populated area of west Texas where a district may encompass several counties, or a densely populated area such as Houston. The application can show underlying boundaries of census blocks or voting precincts if needed. At the bottom of the screen, population and demographic figures for the area being studied will appear; when a legislator takes the mouse and tugs a boundary line over a few streets or precincts, the new demographic and population figures change as well to reflect the new district.

Moreover, a legislator can make maps according to one of those population or demographic characteristics. An attribute of a particular area—the ethnicity of the population, or the district's voting tendencies in past elections—can be used to highlight the area. With several such areas highlighted, a legislator can in effect draw an ideal district—although whether fellow legislators could be persuaded to go along with those boundaries is a question the software can't answer.

The council's RedViewer application is similar to RedAppl in that it can focus on a particular area and jurisdiction in detail, but it does not allow changes to be made. Redistricting proposals up for consideration will be made available through RedViewer on the legislative council's Internet site, and to legislators in their respective chambers.

While many states contract out their redistricting efforts to commercial firms such as Election Data Services, Inc., an ESRI Business Partner and Developer, Texas chose to do its own because of the size of the state and the complexity of the redistricting effort. An earlier version of RedAppl was used for the 1991 redistricting round, but it has undergone considerable upgrading since then, including the addition of MapObjects technology. The council got plenty of experience refining its redistricting tools during the decade, because court

In this sample RedAppl application, an area of Congressional District 10 in Travis County, outlined by the faint triangle, is pulled into the adjoining district, 14. At the bottom of the screen, boxes show a few of the population variables that will be available to members, such as voting age population (VAP), percentage of deviation from ideal district size (%DEV-E), and index percentage that voted Republican statewide in 1998 (IND98G-R). This data is hypothetical, and legislators will be able to view many other variables in the final product.

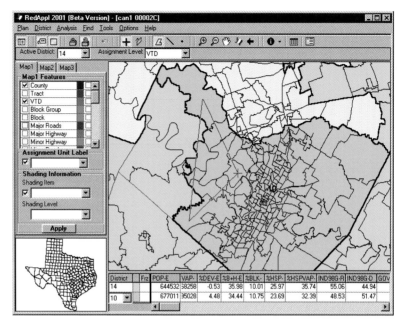

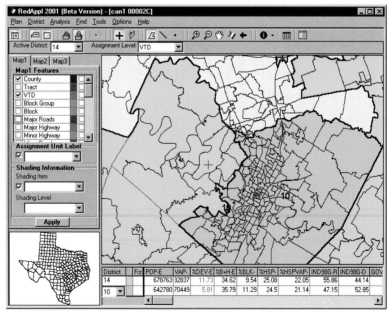

challenges kept the legislature working at it until 1997.

Alan Ware, the redistricting program manager, says GIS will help assure that there won't be any delays this time around—or at least delays caused by the council's technology.

"Our goal is make it so there are no technical obstacles to doing whatever they need to do," he says.

*"The Congress, recognizing the impact of man's activity on the natural environment—population growth, high-density urbanization, industrial expansion, resource exploitation, and new and expanding technological advances—and recognizing the importance of restoring and maintaining environmental quality, declares that the Federal Government, in cooperation with State and local governments, and other public and private organizations, [will] use all means and measures to create and maintain conditions under which man and nature can exist in productive harmony. . . ."*

The National Environmental Policy Act of 1969, Title I (excerpt)

# Chapter 4

# Environment

Decades after the first federal
legislation mandated standards
for protecting the planet on which
we live, the environment remains
one of Americans' top concerns.
Managing natural and environmental resources is a task GIS has been
assisting with since its birth, with
the result that environmental
applications are now some of
the most advanced in the GIS
repertoire.

## Clearing the Air

The Clean Air Act that President George Bush signed into law in November 1990 marked an armistice of sorts to months of intense legislative warfare. Capitol Hill veterans said the battles over the myriad provisions of this comprehensive environmental legislation were some of the roughest they had ever seen.

Given its acrimonious birth, it is perhaps not surprising to find a decade later that controversy still lingers over this legislation, even as it has become clear over the years that the law has largely been doing what it was supposed to—make air cleaner in many parts of the nation. One of the more tenacious of the disputes has pitted northeastern states against those in the Midwest, where smokestacks of huge power plants cough up thousands of tons of sooty emissions every year. Prevailing winds push those emissions eastward, fouling the air of New York and New England with pollutants they did not create. Some in the Northeast contend the Clean Air Act has so far failed to correct this fundamental unfairness.

They contend further that a key component of the Clean Air Act, known as $SO_2$ (sulfur dioxide) Allowance Trading, has actually exacerbated the environmental damage their region of the country has suffered. If true, that would constitute a serious flaw in an important piece of federal public policy.

GIS has been deployed to assess this concern. Using ArcView GIS, the Environmental Protection Agency (EPA) analyzed pollution patterns to see whether the innovative but controversial $SO_2$ Allowance Trading program has in reality been doing the reverse of what it was designed to do, as its critics in the Northeast contend.

The use of GIS in this way reflects a maturing of its applicability—GIS is being used not simply to implement an already formulated public policy, but to clarify and assess its effectiveness, and thus guide policy makers.

"The government is often criticized as being just bean counters only," says Rona Birnbaum, chief of the EPA's Acid Rain Assessment and Communications Branch. "What GIS allows us to do is step out of that mode and go beyond the explanation of the national trends in $SO_2$ emissions only. Using GIS, we can further explain the effects of trading on the environment—specifically, is there a regional shifting in $SO_2$ emissions due to trading?"

The 1990 act, technically a series of amendments to the original 1970 legislation, is an excruciatingly detailed document mandating specific ways that specific kinds of pollutants are to be reduced. Among the most notorious of these is acid rain.

A substance as ugly as it sounds, acid rain is a toxic soup of smokestack emissions and atmospheric moisture that falls to earth and eats away at buildings and statues, chews up forests, and poisons lakes and streams. In the 6.5-million-acre

Adirondack Park in upstate New York, for example, lakes that a few dozen years ago were renowned as fabulous fishing spots are now completely empty of fish, and indeed, of much of anything living. Strong feelings about acid rain run deep in this part of the world.

An important ingredient of acid rain is sulfur dioxide. The Clean Air Act ordered that by 2010, the amount of sulfur dioxide emitted nationally should be half of what it was in 1980. Another significant acid rain ingredient, nitrogen oxide, was the focus of a separate provision of the act.

What was innovative about the act's mandate was the way this reduction was to be achieved. The legislation ordered an overall, national reduction in sulfur dioxide emissions. Individual sulfur dioxide producers were allotted a certain number of tons—known as their allowances—that they were permitted to emit. But just how they reduced their own sulfur dioxide emissions to achieve the national reduction was up to them. They could use cleaner-burning fuel. They could install pollution-control technology. They could tear down old, inefficient plants and build new, efficient ones. And they could trade their sulfur dioxide allowances among themselves within the $SO_2$ Allowance Trading system.

Allowance trading works by allowing those plants that emit less than their allowed annual tonnage of sulfur dioxide to bank the extra—that is, they can keep their unused tons on the books and use them in a later year. They also can sell

Gary Randorf/Adirondack Council

Adirondack Park, seen here from the top of Gothics, has been hard hit by the effects of acid rain.

the extras to other utilities that may need more than their year's allotment. Extra allowances also can be sold to the highest bidder at auction. The allowance-trading rationale was that the marketplace—supply and demand—would provide an incentive to utilities to find ways to keep their emissions low. Either the cost of buying extra tons would be too high, or the money to be saved by reducing emissions was too great an incentive to be ignored. In addition, because all the federal government does is cap the $SO_2$ emissions nationally, throwing the burden of compliance onto the utilities saves the government administrative costs.

The underlying concept was not a new one, and allowance trading was endorsed by both business and environmental groups as a workable, indeed ingenious, economic solution. It stirred controversy anyway. Its critics said it was no more than a fancy way for polluters to buy their way out of their own messes. Some scoffed at the notion that something as amorphous as the right to pollute could be a commodity as tangible as oats or pork bellies. The EPA's response was that it was the right *not* to pollute that was the commodity.

Measurable success began to be seen almost immediately. For example, the national cap on 1996 sulfur dioxide emissions was 8.3 million tons. Actual 1996 emissions amounted to only 5.4 million tons. Moreover, because so many unused allowances were carried over from 1995, the legal 1996 limit was 11.7 million tons. Although there were increases in sulfur dioxide emissions in individual states, and in individual utilities, it was clear that overall emissions had gone down. And program costs were less than critics had feared.

Despite such success, applause for the acid rain program has been far from universal, especially in the Northeast. Studies showed that acid rain was harming sensitive regions such as the Adirondacks and the Catskills more than had been expected. The allowance trading program was particularly troublesome to New Yorkers. New York utilities already had to follow more stringent state emissions guidelines. Therefore, under the federal allowance trading rules, New York State utilities had more allowances than they needed, which they were free to sell or trade to anybody they wanted—including to utilities in the Midwest whose emissions were blowing back over New York.

The result: extra allowances in New York could mean extra acid rain in New York, too—in effect adding injury—a self-inflicted one—to insult, in the eyes of many New Yorkers. And in fact in 1993, one of New York's large utilities, the Long Island Lighting Co., disclosed that it had indeed sold options on some of its extra allowances to a fossil-fuel supplier with several Midwest power plant clients. (Five years later, the utility agreed to abide by state restrictions on its allowance trading, although some said the agreement was more symbolic than practical.)

The same year, New York State and some environmental organizations took the EPA to court, while legislators in Albany began drafting restrictive state allowance trading laws.

It was against this complex background that EPA environmental policy analyst Jennifer Kramer began in 1998 to try to determine whether the allowance trading program was in fact working against the intent of the Clean Air Act. Her investigative tool was ArcView GIS.

Kramer first identified which plants had bought allowances in excess of that year's allocation. She then identified the sources of those additional allowances. She discounted intervening trades on the grounds that an intervening trade had no actual environmental effect; that is, a transaction in which a plant in Ohio acquired extra allowances from a plant in Florida, which had in turn acquired them from a New York plant, would be counted as a net exchange from New York to Ohio.

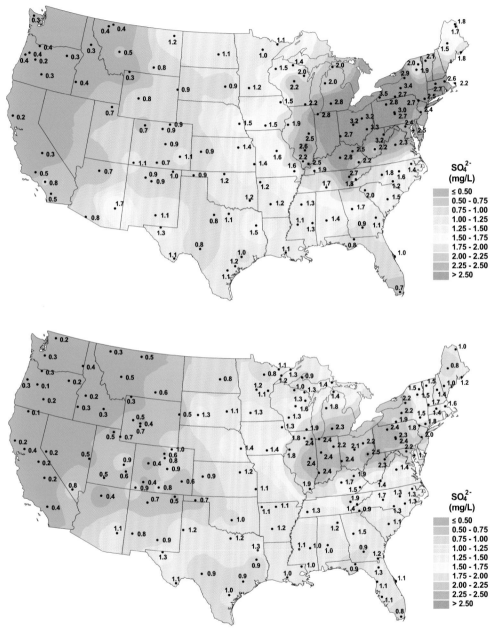

Maps from the National Atmospheric Deposition Program, created with ESRI software, show clearly how deposits of sulfates from acid rain are concentrated in the Midwest and Northeast. They also indicate how those deposits have declined dramatically over the 15-year period from 1985, top, to 1998, bottom. Despite this and other evidence that the Clean Air Act is working, scientists say acid levels in areas of New York such as the Adirondacks remain disturbingly high, and these areas may take longer than expected to recover from the effects of acid rain.

Kramer then wrote a script in Avenue™, the ArcView GIS programming language, that calculated the geographic mean centers of trading activity, both buying and selling, for the first three years of the SO$_2$ allowance trading program, 1995 through 1997. The calculation was weighted; those plants that acquired or supplied allowances more heavily would push or pull the centers accordingly.

Presumably, since midwestern power plants were doing most of the emitting of pollutants, the center of buying activity, of acquiring extra allowances, would also be located in the Midwest. And in fact, Kramer's analysis showed this to be the case.

Presumably also, if northeastern plants were the ones supplying most of the allowances that those midwestern plants needed—meaning northeastern utilities were supplying the allowances that caused more sulfur dioxide to blow back on them—the center of supplying activity would be skewed toward the Northeast.

Environmental Analyst Jennifer Kramer showed that the geographic mean centers of supplying and acquiring activity of sulfur dioxide allowances did not shift greatly during the first three years of the program.

## Allowance Trading Activity 1995-1997
### Geographic Mean Centers of SO2 Allowance Trading

1995 Acquiring Activity

1996 Acquiring Activity

1997 Acquiring Activity

Plants Acquiring Additional Allowances
- 1-25781
- 25782-51563
- 51564-103125
- 103126-206250
- 206251-275000

Plants Supplying Additional Allowances
- 1-61250
- 61251-122500
- 122501-245000
- 245001-367500
- 367501-490000

1995 Supplying Activity

1996 Supplying Activity

1997 Supplying Activity

ACID RAIN PROGRAM

Kramer's analysis showed that this was definitely *not* the case.

"The analysis revealed that the overwhelming majority of allowances were retired in the same state in which they were originally allocated," Kramer wrote in a paper given at the 1999 ESRI International User Conference. "The geographic centers of trading were very close to each other (within approximately 200 miles), and remained concentrated in the Midwest for all three years. . . . Ecologically significant regional shifting in emissions is not occurring; the analysis argues against the need for safeguards to control or limit allowance trading."

Moreover, the EPA points out, although most of the acquiring activity takes place in the Midwest, some of the most significant reductions in $SO_2$ emissions have also taken place there.

"We are fairly comfortably able to say that we're not seeing any significant emissions shifting because of allowance trading," says Birnbaum, the EPA Acid Rain Assessment and Communications branch chief.

The EPA's GIS analysis is but a small portion of a voluminous amount of study on acid rain itself, its effects, and the federal government's efforts to deal with it. It is a limited analysis, since it deals with only three years' worth of data, and focuses strictly on buying and selling of extra allowances.

And while it is one of many studies that show that the hard-fought clean air legislation is by and large a public policy success, other studies have come to more

ambivalent conclusions. One of the most definitive of them, published in a 1999 issue of the journal *Nature,* showed that efforts to reduce acid rain are working, but also that recovery from decades of damage—particularly in the Adirondack region—will take much longer than expected. Another study in 2000 by the General Accounting Office pointed out that utilities in New York State had, from 1995 to 1998, sold more than two-and-a-half times as many allowances outside the state as they had bought; but it also said sulfate levels in Adirondack lakes had in general diminished since the Clean Air Act went into effect.

New York State activists say that although their early fears about allowance trading may have diminished somewhat, they believe more stringent acid rain rules are nonetheless still needed to protect areas such as the Adirondacks. Whatever the merits of the GIS study, the EPA is still not doing enough to prevent the destruction of New York's natural resources by utilities hundreds of miles away, in their view.

But the ArcView GIS analysis may also mark the beginning of a new system for assessing environmental damage—especially if the success of allowance trading encourages policy makers to apply that system to other environmental policy areas. Sulfur dioxide is only one of many substances the public is deciding it can do without.

In environmental public policy, GIS has helped clear the air—both literally and politically.

## Breaking Through a Brick Wall

MASSACHUSETTS RESIDENTS might be in the middle of an east–west water war rivaling California's north–south version were it not for the role GIS played in the treaty that settled it. That treaty, more formally called the Watershed Protection Act, took years to pass—and did so only after GIS technology clearly showed its opponents that the legislation would not do the kind of harm they had feared. And GIS has continued in succeeding years to help keep the peace in Massachusetts.

In the late 1970s and early 1980s, dire warnings began to be heard in the Commonwealth that Metropolitan Boston's water supply would not last very far into the 21st century. Boston's water was not, like most other large American cities, drawn from a huge mechanical treatment system. Instead, it came mostly from two large reservoirs, the Quabbin and the Wachusett, located in the central part of the state. It was extraordinarily clean water.

Among the ideas for maintaining this supply of clean water that were heard was one to divert water from western and central Massachusetts rivers, such as the Connecticut, into the reservoirs. Those who lived in western and central Massachusetts didn't like that idea at all. Nor did environmentalists such as the Massachusetts Audubon Society's Robie Hubley. Hubley, the group's long-time legislative director, argued that simple conservation measures would go a long way toward solving the problem; a study a few years later bore out his reasoning.

A corollary of Hubley's conservation idea was protection: the watershed around the reservoirs could be protected from contaminants by placing restrictions on development and other kinds of activity. There was already concern about development beginning to crowd in on the Wachusett, and the idea took on a certain currency.

So in 1987, state Representative David Cohen of the Boston suburb of Newton introduced legislation to establish buffer zones around the watersheds. Cohen's proposal would restrict development in some watershed areas and provide money for the Commonwealth to protect other watershed land by buying it outright.

The bill hit a brick wall.

Some of the opposition came from those who simply disliked the notion of the government taking land, even for the public good. But more significant was the opposition from the central and western part of the state, where it was not at all clear which landowners would be restricted from developing their lands. Nor was it clear which portions of local towns would fall within the watershed buffer zones, restricting development within them, and therefore restricting potential property and sales taxes. The available maps couldn't answer these questions. Not unnaturally, nervous—and angry— property owners and local officials in central and western Massachusetts conveyed their feelings to their representatives at the statehouse. At one community meeting Cohen held in the central Massachusetts town of Princeton, someone showed up with real tar and real feathers, and had to be physically restrained.

"The maps we used were really approximations," says Cohen, now mayor of Newton. "We were using anything we could get our hands on, but we didn't have an accurate map for the first couple of years we were trying to do this."

That lack of information resulted not just in opposition, but in wild speculation about the arbitrary, capricious government land grabs that were sure to result; no information meant misinformation, and that hardened opposition.

"There were no numbers," says Christian Jacqz, then a GIS analyst with the Commonwealth. "People were saying, jeez, we'll never be able to build anything."

Then, the federal Environmental Protection Agency invited itself into the discussions. Recently passed amendments to the federal Safe Drinking Water Act required that, with few exceptions, all surface water supplies in the country be filtered. The Commonwealth wanted its Boston water system to be one of those exceptions. Its argument was that because the water supply was already so clean, the kind of filtration system the EPA was talking about requiring, and which might cost more than $1 billion, wasn't needed. Without making any promises, the EPA indicated it might be willing to grant the Commonwealth a waiver to the Safe Water Drinking Act if a way was found to protect the watershed.

Despite this added impetus, Cohen's bill kept running into that brick wall, year after year.

Robie Hubley gave Cohen a copy of a book he liked a lot: Ian McHarg's *Design With Nature,* a seminal work about the interaction of man-made and natural environments, and about how the two need not be mutually exclusive. Hubley, being well informed on such issues, had also been hearing about a new technology called GIS, and what it was capable of doing. Through a circuitous route, Cohen also heard about GIS. Let's give it a try, he said.

The state's GIS program (MassGIS) at that point consisted of three people, including Jacqz, housed within the Executive Office of Environmental Affairs. They were working on a project with the United States Geological Survey, finding potential sites for hazardous-waste facilities. The group's leader at the time, Michael Terner, says the request from Cohen for help was a fortuitous one, since the group was already ahead of schedule on its federal project, and already working with Massachusetts hydrological data. And they were definitely keeping an eye out for new projects that would raise the visibility of GIS.

Using ArcInfo, MassGIS team members created digital maps of the watershed, the reservoirs, and the tributaries in question. Then they created 200- and 400-foot buffers around the reservoirs and tributaries, a huge, cumbersome set of computations that can be done by ArcInfo with a single command. ArcInfo also quickly calculated the total area of the buffers, a task that on a paper map is also laborious and time-consuming. Once they had the total protected area calculated, they began subtracting from it; much land was already protected, or already owned by the Commonwealth, so it

> *GIS makes things graphic, which is the way the human brain works, so the connections are so perfectly obvious.*
>
> **ROBIE HUBLEY, MASSACHUSETTS AUDUBON SOCIETY**

could not be counted as new land that was going to be restricted from development. They then overlaid a land-use map and subtracted even more land from the protected zone: land that already had development on it would be grandfathered in by the legislation.

Lastly, they overlaid maps of town boundaries to see just how much of a particular town's base of developable land might be taken out of circulation by the legislation.

The new maps showed that only small percentages of the total land within the boundaries of many towns would be affected—much smaller than the rumor mill had been speculating.

Terner, who later helped found Boston-based Applied Geographics, Inc., says the team carefully put together poster-sized paper maps of their analyses, which had taken less than a month to do. Then Cohen and his aides took them around

to the affected central Massachusetts towns. The results were dramatic.

"The opposition basically vanished," says Hubley. Why is not hard to understand, he says. "GIS makes things graphic, which is the way the human brain works, so the connections are so perfectly obvious."

"It was finally after we got the GIS maps that we were able to show people how their land was being impacted," Cohen concurs, "and that made it much easier to sell the bill, because the issue of fairness and arbitrariness was taken away."

"It changed the dynamics of the debate," says David Barenberg, one of Cohen's aides at the time, "so that it was fact-based instead of based on rhetoric." Moreover, once the affected residents were identified accurately through the maps, it allowed the legislation to be more finely tuned. Specifically, it allowed the bill's writers to make a distinction between commercial land development— which they wanted to restrict—and smaller, noncommercial development that was intended to benefit only the landowner and his or her family, and which they did not want to restrict.

The Cohen bill, aka the Watershed Protection Act, finally got the votes it needed for passage in the spring of 1992 and was signed into law by Governor William Weld. It said there could be no development of any kind within 400 feet of the Quabbin and Wachusett reservoirs, nor within 200 feet of their tributaries. Development was restricted between 200 and 400 feet of tributaries.

The bill also authorized $135 million to buy land. Property owners were guaranteed notifications and hearings and appeals, and there were numerous exemptions and exceptions.

Although the new GIS maps could not be given all the credit for the bill's passage—the EPA's threat contributed—those involved say it was essential to its final passage.

In that regard, Massachusetts' experience is cutting-edge. Most of the time, when GIS meets public policy, GIS helps implement that public policy. In Massachusetts' case, GIS helped create that policy and make it a reality.

GIS innovations in Massachusetts have continued to expand the parameters of policy making.

For example, GIS was used in the language of watershed legislation itself to define the areas that were the subject of the law, one of the first times this was ever done. Traditionally, legislation written to define a land area will do so by reference to geographic coordinates, property records, vegetation or soil type, or description of soil features. The Massachusetts legislation directed that the "location of tributaries and surface waters shall be determined by reference to maps generated by the Massachusetts geographic information service." As GIS becomes more and more integrated into the legislative process, such definitions are likely to become more commonplace.

GIS in this new legislative context can bring new problems that policy makers will have to overcome. For example, the

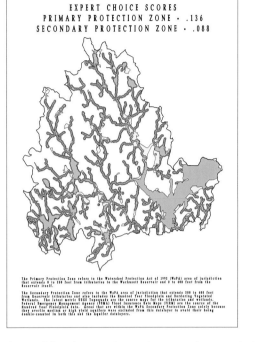

A map of the primary and secondary protection zones in the Wachusett Reservoir watershed. The orange-tinted primary zones are lands within 400 feet of the reservoir and 200 feet of its tributaries where no development may occur. The yellow secondary zones are between 200 and 400 feet of the reservoirs' tributaries, and some limited development may occur within those areas.

maps put together to show local towns the boundaries of the watershed bill were accurate enough for that limited display purpose. Many assumed they would also be used to carry out the bill's dictates. But they were not detailed or accurate enough to be used for the kind of parcel-by-parcel, legally binding decisions that would have to be made later. This was a point that took some effort to get people

*It was finally after we got the GIS maps that we were able to show people how their land was being impacted, and that made it much easier to sell the bill, because the issue of fairness and arbitrariness was taken away.*

**DAVID COHEN, MAYOR, NEWTON, MASSACHUSETTS**

to understand. "I wrote a lot of memos back then, saying, wait, you can't do this," says Jacqz, who later became director of MassGIS.

In the end, the law's language directed that the underlying basemap for the watershed protection law would be 1:25,000-scale maps, more detailed than those that were used for lobbying in the affected towns. But even these sometimes don't show certain areas with enough accuracy; some tributaries that exist aren't shown on them. Whenever there is a question, field inspections are done.

GIS has continued to be an essential part of the effort by the Commonwealth to identify land within the Wachusett watershed that should be protected. Paul Penner, GIS coordinator for the Metropolitan District Commission's Division of Watershed Management, and his staff developed a unique land-buying model in ArcInfo to guide those decisions.

First, Penner and his staff considered all the attributes of a piece of land that might make it one the Commonwealth should buy to protect it from development; after much discussion, they whittled the list down to 12 that could be mapped. These criteria included such

factors as a parcel's distance to a tributary or a reservoir, naturally; its proximity to 100-year floodplains, since a flood would likely wash contaminants into the reservoirs; and whether the land contained steep slopes, since such land would be more subject to erosion, and thus also more likely to wash contaminants into the reservoirs. Using decision-making software from Expert Choice, Inc., they assigned a score to each of these 12 criteria.

In ArcInfo, they created a layer for each of these. For each piece of land in the watershed that met a particular criterion, a polygon was created. Each of these was assigned to the appropriate layer. Then all the layers were combined. The scores of overlapping polygons—that is, a piece of land that appeared in two or more data layers because it met two or more of the criteria—were added together. With some further refinements, the agency wound up with a complete map of the available land ranked in order of its importance for acquisition. Land that met several criteria became higher priority land to buy.

Other kinds of analyses could be done from this model. A prime example was

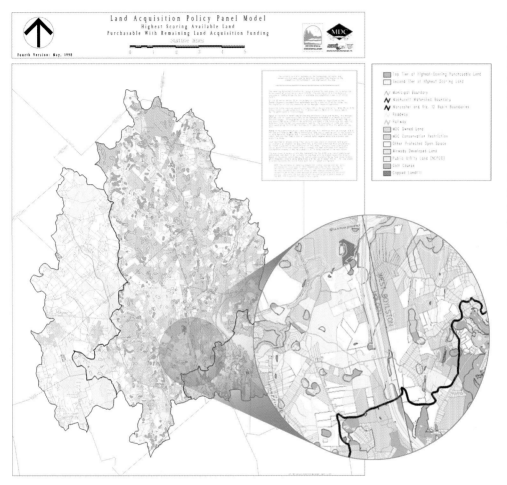

one Penner did for the continuing dispute with the EPA—which had developed into full-blown federal litigation. Among many other issues in dispute, the Commonwealth had asked for a waiver of federal regulations regarding the way it would have to treat the water destined for Greater Boston. To get that waiver, the Commonwealth had to meet certain requirements, and the EPA contended it had not met all of them.

One requirement was that the Commonwealth buy 25 percent of the Wachusett Reservoir watershed by 1998. The state conceded it had narrowly missed the deadline. But it argued that the EPA's 25-percent figure counted all watershed land equally, regardless of its potential to affect water quality. When Penner did an analysis of the quality of the land purchases using the ArcInfo model, he showed that the Commonwealth had, by the deadline, controlled lands most critical to the health and safety of the drinking water supply. Using GIS, the state had made more reasoned land acquisition decisions that fulfilled the spirit of the waiver requirement—to protect the watershed.

Massachusetts is one of the oldest settled areas of the country, but its innovative use of GIS in public policy may be giving the rest of the country a glimpse of the future.

"... security was attained in the earlier days through the interdependence of members of families upon each other and of the families within a small community upon each other. The complexities of great communities and of organized industry make less real these simple means of security. Therefore, we are compelled to employ the active interest of the Nation as a whole through government in order to encourage a greater security for each individual who composes it."

Franklin D. Roosevelt: Message of the President to Congress, June 8, 1934

*Chapter 5*

# Social Services

Few would argue against a government's fundamental duty to provide help of some kind to those who cannot help themselves. It is over the questions of how and to what degree that disputes arise. GIS is helping to focus some of these questions and streamline the delivery of services, with the result that some of the most innovative GIS work is being done in this arena.

## Mapping Truths, Mapping Needs

GIS HAS LONG BEEN ASSOCIATED with the inanimate: land and its use, water resources and systems, transportation networks, to mention only a few. But recently, those whose job it is to help people are finding in GIS a powerful tool for mapping and analyzing social problems.

Some say GIS can transform the way social programs and services are designed and carried out in this country.

Anita Bock is one. Bock headed the Miami office of Florida's Department of Children and Families through most of the 1990s. District 11, covering Miami–Dade and Monroe counties, was responsible for helping people across the whole South Florida spectrum of social issues and problems, including welfare reform, foster care, refugee assistance, child abuse, and elder abuse.

Bock carried a bag full of GIS-based maps and charts around under her arm so often and to so many places, it became something of a trademark: here comes Anita and her maps, they'd say. She took them to Chamber of Commerce meetings, to United Way presentations, to meetings with bankers and lawyers, to sessions of the Miami–Dade County Commission, and to Tallahassee when it came time to talk to state legislators.

She did so because GIS showed South Florida's social problems so graphically, making people understand the breadth of those problems in a way that Bock had never been able to get across to them before.

"I consider it to be one of the most significant things I've ever worked on," says Bock, now the director of Los Angeles County's Department of Children and Family Services. "It absolutely revolutionized the way we did business."

Bock is not alone. A growing number of social services practitioners across the nation are discovering in GIS a new way to help people understand social problems, to show legislators and constituents alike the wide discrepancies between needs and resources, and to place those resources in communities.

"The demand and the interest and the possibilities of this stuff—the sky's the limit," says Pat McGuigan of Rhode Island's The Providence Plan, a nonprofit group also using GIS to map problems and resources.

From the outside, the concept seems almost unconscionably simplistic: merely showing on a map that some places have more or fewer problems, or problems different from other places, seems to belabor the obvious.

Except that before GIS technology, nothing comparable has existed in the world of social services. There were only other, more limited ways of presenting the state of a city: statistics and raw numbers, which put people to sleep; anecdotes, which don't put people to sleep, but aren't definitive either; and charts, which are definitive, but can't show you where a problem is occurring.

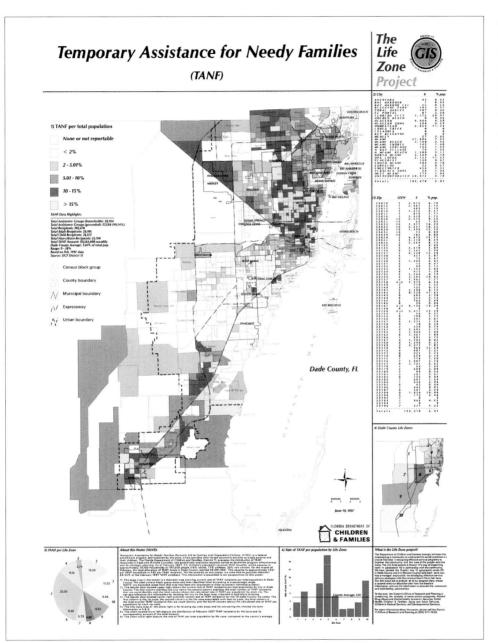

A District 11 map shows the distribution of Temporary Aid to Needy Families, formerly known as AFDC, throughout Miami–Dade County.

*I consider it to be one of the most significant things I've
ever worked on. [GIS] absolutely revolutionized the way
we did business.*

**ANITA BOCK, DIRECTOR, LOS ANGELES COUNTY DEPARTMENT OF CHILDREN AND FAMILY SERVICES**

Andrew Dickman, the District 11 Director of Research and Community Affairs, likens GIS technology now to the late 19th- and early 20th-century breakthroughs in photographic technology. These allowed photographer Jacob Riis for the first time to show newspaper readers the graphic horrors of New York City slum life, which in turn helped fuel reform efforts.

The GIS maps were graphic enough in South Florida to help one Miami–Dade County commissioner, Barbara Carey–Schuler, pry loose some extra funding for

This Providence Plan map of lead-poisoning rates among children in the city is typical of the kind of graphic portrayal of community physical and social health that can be done with neighborhood indicator data. Such a map can help providers of service, such as medical care, target those services more efficiently.

**Incidence of Elevated Blood Lead Levels (≥10µg/dl) Among Providence Children**

Wanskuck · Charles · Hope · Elmhurst · Mount Hope · Blackstone · Mount Pleasant · Manton · Smith Hill · Valley · College Hill · Wayland · Downtown · Olneyville · Federal Hill · Fox Point · Hartford · Upper South Providence · Silver Lake · West End · Lower South Providence · Elmwood · Reservoir · Washington Park · South Elmwood

**Providence Children Tested in 1998: 8,191**

**Providence Children with lead poisoning: 1,625 (20%)**

Poisonings per census tract

- 0-25 children
- 26-50 children
- 51-100 children
- 101-167 children

Data Source: Rhode Island Department of Health

Map Produced by The Providence Plan for the Mayor's Early Childhood Task Force, January 2000

*When they went out into the Life Zones to show real people what was going on, the response was positive: "Thank God, somebody's telling us the truth."*

**ANDREW DICKMAN, DISTRICT 11 DIRECTOR OF RESEARCH AND COMMUNITY AFFAIRS**

the area she represented. A set of maps District 11 put together for the Miami–Dade County Social Services Master Plan showed that poverty and other problems were so serious in Carey–Schuler's district that she was able in 1998 to convince her fellow commissioners to allocate an extra $2 million in general funds for her constituents.

Those who are pursuing the GIS cause, such as District 11 and The Providence Plan and a handful of others, have banded together under the umbrella of the National Neighborhood Indicators Project (NNIP) of the Urban Institute, a nonpartisan Washington, D.C., policy research organization.

Neighborhood indicators are the equivalent of economic indicators such as the GNP, except they measure a community's social health. Indicators can include measures of how well or how badly people are living, and the physical conditions they live in. Poverty, unemployment, housing code violations, high school drop-out rates, communicable diseases, babies with low birth weights, crime rates, liquor licenses, public transit availability, and many others are all pieces of data—indicators—that can be mapped in a GIS, then compared to other indicators, and to available resources.

This kind of mapping advances some distinct public policy priorities.

One is finding a common ground: regardless of ideology, being able to see—quite literally—where a government program is working and where it is not provides a common basis for further discussion.

Another is devolution, the politically popular push to bring decision making down the policy food chain to the local level.

That in turn leads to a third priority, the empowerment of communities: a neighborhood with a better grasp of its problems is in a better position to make decisions about how to solve them.

"To make real change, we think you get this stuff in the hands of folks, and they'll hold public agencies accountable, or take on the problem themselves," says Patrick Burke, manager of another NNIP partner organization, the Atlanta Project's office of Data and Policy Analysis (DAPA).

While the use of GIS to help communities is still relatively new, theories of what is called Public Participation GIS are not. The subject has been the topic of many academic papers and conferences under the aegis of Project Varenius of the National Center for Geographic Information and Analysis.

South Florida's experience is particularly instructive because Bock and Dickman, the agency's urban planning and GIS specialist, set out to change things within the social services system itself, rather than from an outside nonprofit or academic setting. Their work grew out of the effects of a natural disaster, Hurricane Andrew, which in 1992 devastated South Florida. Because Andrew's destruction cut across bureaucratic and agency lines, teams of social service and public health professionals, who came to be known as Community Health Action Teams (CHAT), were formed to visit hard-hit areas, to figure out who needed what help where, and to expedite that help, regardless of which bureaucracy was technically responsible for services. Using ArcInfo and ArcView GIS under a grant from the Centers for Disease Control and Prevention, Dickman was gathering data and helping map areas where the teams needed to visit and help.

Bock, a corporate lawyer recently hired to run District 11, found what Dickman was doing so fascinating that she put him to work incorporating GIS into the office's planning and research activities, of which there were none up to that point. Nor, in fact, were there any funds set aside by Tallahassee for such activities. So Bock stitched together money from various sources, including her own administrative budget, to bring both planning and GIS functions into the agency.

Seeing how effective the CHAT system had been at delivering services based on geography, Bock and Dickman devised a way to deliver all District 11 social services by geographic regions, which they called Life Zones. Miami–Dade County was divided into 10 of them, and they cut across traditional administrative groupings. Life Zones were roughly equal in population, with each zone's manager responsible for overseeing all social services within a region.

This was a break from the traditional way social services are distributed, in Florida and elsewhere. Traditionally, money is doled out by the state legislature for a particular social program. It is a vertical system. The money to solve each problem trickles down through different bureaucracies, separate from each other: child abuse funds are separate from teen pregnancy funds, which are separate from refugee assistance funds. Moreover, child abuse managers rarely speak to teen pregnancy managers or to refugee assistance managers.

In Bock's view, this traditional bureaucratic separation wasn't working then and doesn't now; all social dysfunction is interrelated.

"My goal was to completely decentralize management, to actually start allowing communities to look at their top 10 social concerns and to decide where they wanted their money spent," she says.

Dickman's GIS department, using ArcView GIS and ArcInfo software, took department client records already in the department's possession and matched the address of a client to the appropriate Life Zone. Neighborhoods were labeled as such, because neighborhoods are how

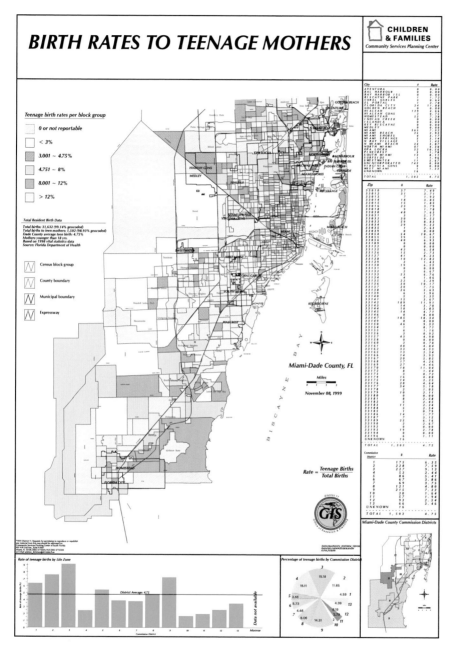

An example of the kind of poster Anita Bock took with her everywhere. The teen birth rate in Miami–Dade by block group is shown on the main map; neighborhood names are in light green. The color yellow indicates where the teen birth rate is highest. The data is also broken down by commission district, by city, by ZIP Code, and by Life Zone.

people really think of where they live, in Bock's view.

The GIS department created thematic maps that showed the intensity of social and health problems within Life Zones, such as teen pregnancy, AIDS cases, and drug and alcohol addiction. Similar Life Zone maps were created showing how resources such as mental health counseling or food stamp offices, day-care centers, public health clinics, or public transportation routes were distributed. When matched against the maps of social problems, the disparity between need and resource was in many cases made graphically obvious.

This kind of disparity is particularly relevant in the era of welfare reform. Several NNIP partner agencies have mapped the locations of areas with high numbers of welfare recipients who are scheduled to lose their benefits by a statutory deadline, and the location of schools and jobs. In many areas, the inadequacy of public transportation in welfare-to-work programs has become obvious.

People at first resisted the graphic portrayal of their neighborhood problems. Bock, whose name was usually preceded by the adjective "outspoken" in newspaper accounts, was accused of trying to stigmatize neighborhoods by pointing out the depth and breadth of their social problems. But after a time, people saw the value in the maps and charts, Bock says. While they pinpointed problems, they also helped define for neighborhoods and community leaders which problems they needed to concentrate on, and those on which they need not waste energy or resources.

"When they went out into the Life Zones to show real people what was going on, the response was positive," says Dickman: "'Thank God, somebody's telling us the truth.'"

There were some surprises. For example, the Life Zone maps showed that a disproportionate number of temporary foster homes, where abused children were placed until their cases were settled, were concentrated in the northwest section of Miami–Dade County. As it happened, many of the department's own employees lived in the same area. Some were, in fact, doubling as temporary foster parents. That told the department that word-of-mouth was a principal method of foster home recruitment, and that was not a method they wanted to use. It told them also that new recruitment efforts were needed, and it told them they needed to disperse foster homes through a wider area.

Another lesson was an organizational one. Dickman says that having the GIS department physically close to the executive offices was important in the early years of setting up the program. Neighborhood indicator data is often sensitive data, and other departments were resistant to releasing it to some new program they had never heard of. Having Bock and the department's legal counsel physically close to the executive office, to verify the legitimacy of a request when necessary, helped get those requests filled, and to give the GIS program credibility, Dickman says.

But not everybody liked Life Zones, or even mapping social problems, says Bock, with customary bluntness.

"You could see the progression of the blight throughout Dade County," she says. "It was abundantly clear to everybody that the entire fabric of our community was unraveling in many areas.

"The Chamber of Commerce was very uncomfortable with my presentations. This wasn't the Miami that they wanted to portray."

Problems arose also from within the organization, where managers assigned to administer the Life Zones had to keep the traditional, vertical organization going at the same time. It was a lot of extra work they did not get paid extra to do. So for those reasons, a full conversion of the office's organization to the Life Zones concept never took place, although it remains as a planning tool. And after the 1998 election brought a new chief executive to Florida, Bock departed.

But GIS remains behind, firmly established as a part of South Florida's social services system. District 11's planning and research operations, now known as the Community Services Planning Center, has built a reputation. Demand for their products, such as maps of neighborhood resources, is so strong they have largely automated the production process using ESRI's ARC Macro Language. The center has also helped its own cause by contracting for outside work from local organizations such as the United Way, and with national ones such as the Manpower Demonstration Research Corporation, to create maps and other products.

Bock says she intends to spread the word of GIS in social services from her new post in California. Its potential is too big to ignore, she says.

"It had a profound influence on the way I did business in Miami," she says, "and I have every expectation that that will be the same here in L.A."

## Older Drivers, New Approach

IN GEORGIA, a 97-year-old driver accidentally runs down a roadside flagman. In San Francisco, a 71-year-old driver hits two small children. In Maine, an 87-year-old driver panics in a parking lot and drives right through the wall of a restaurant.

News stories such as these, which appeared within weeks of each other in 1999, are frequently succeeded by angry letters to the editor, demanding a fast, tough solution to the problem of these dangerous elderly drivers: do something, they say, but get these old folks off the roads.

Just how these grandmothers and grandfathers are to continue the day-to-day business of life—getting to the doctor, to the supermarket, to their kids' houses—without a car is a question neither posed nor answered by the letter writers. Fast, tough solutions are rarely complete solutions.

Clearly, some elderly drivers should not be behind the wheel. When we age, we don't see as well, we don't hear as well, and our bodies can't twist and turn the way they once could, the way they need to for safe driving. State governments are trying to deal with the issue variously: some are considering imposing additional driver's license testing requirements, while others are beefing up systems that encourage people to report unsafe driving incidents.

But a small nonprofit organization in Maine is putting together an entirely different, innovative solution to the problem, with the help of GIS technology. The Independent Transportation Network (ITN) of Portland, Maine, has come up with a system that allows older folks whose driving days are over to get around town with the kind of freedom they once had when they were driving. It is a ride-sharing system with a difference. It is economically self-sufficient, and thus, replicable anywhere across the nation.

The ITN solution may have arrived not a moment too soon, given the crisis that looms when two late 20th-century trends converge early in the 21st.

In the same way they created a demographic bulge of youth in the 1960s and 1970s, the Baby Boomers are poised to create another, aging bulge. From 1995 to 2010 the number of Americans aged 65 or older will increase by about 17 percent, from 33.5 million to 39.4 million; in the succeeding two decades, that number will grow by 75 percent to more than 69 million.

On a collision course with that trend is the continuing American addiction to the automobile. In 1960, Americans drove slightly less than 600,000 miles in their cars. By 1990, the figure was close to 2 million, and by 1996, more than 2.2 million. There seems to be no serious alternative to the automobile on America's transportation horizon.

So as millions of baby boomers begin to grow old and frail, they will do so in a land ever more dependent on cars. By

2020, it is estimated there will be more than 40 million drivers over the age of 70.

"We are not, as a country, planning for this," warns Katherine Freund, who is. Freund founded the ITN in Portland, and invented its unique ride-share system.

Freund, who has a master's degree in public policy, did extensive research into the problem and found that to give up driving means giving up much more than most people realize. Those quintessentially American traits of independence and self-sufficiency are the first to be abandoned when you can no longer drive. They are also the hardest. Should you be lucky enough to have adult children and friends living nearby, you must start asking for favors. Living near a bus line helps, sort of, since you can take the bus to the supermarket. But then you can carry home only one bag at a time, so you have to go several times a week. You must time the trip so that it coincides with the hours in a day when you have some energy, and only when it's not icy and snowy because then you could fall. Falls can be catastrophic when you're old. One result of all these barriers to mobility is that the elderly become more and more isolated, also with catastrophic results.

Government-sponsored alternatives were in many ways no better, Freund found. They usually involved mass transit with its own particular limitations; besides, two-thirds of elderly Americans live in suburban and semirural areas, where mass transit is at best a hit-or-miss proposition.

In Portland, the ITN distills many of these lessons, and incorporates the freedoms afforded by a car. Its basic operation is simple: seniors in Portland who need transportation simply join the ITN and set up an account. When they need a ride somewhere, they call; a driver is dispatched, picks them up, and takes them where they want to go. The cost is deducted from their account.

The ITN gives riders a choice about how they will ride, and how much they spend. If they are willing to split a car and driver with other people, the ride will cost less. If they are willing to schedule ahead of time, they'll get another discount. If they can be flexible about when they get picked up and when they get dropped off, that can save money too.

The independence the system guarantees is why it has succeeded and why Freund believes it can work anywhere. Managing freedom, however, is a complex, labor-intensive business, one that, in order to work at maximum efficiency, requires a technological solution.

Freund has found that solution in GIS and at GeoFields, Inc., an Atlanta-based applications-development consulting firm and ESRI Business Partner. A GIS solution was needed because of the sheer quantity of data that ITN dispatchers and administrators must juggle. They need to keep track of destinations, time windows, road detours and closures; whether riders want to share a ride with one person, or two or three, and whether those three are their friends or strangers; how much to charge each rider for each segment of each journey, and whether that segment is shared by other riders, and by how many; and whether the driver is a volunteer or paid.

The system GeoFields is designing for ITN keeps track of drivers and riders in a relational database. For the complex logistical work, GeoFields is deploying NetEngine™, an ESRI developer tool specifically designed to do the kind of network analysis that ITN requires. NetEngine programs store and manipulate very large networks, which is what street systems are. NetEngine calculates complex mathematical problems known as algorithms, which are needed to figure out the cheapest, fastest, or most efficient route from point A to point B, when

there are many other variables between A and B. These are exactly the kinds of routing problems ITN faces every day—for example, finding the quickest way to route an elderly rider wanting to go to the supermarket every Tuesday at 10 A.M. but also wanting to share the ride with a friend from across town, and who can leave as late as 10:35, but who must be back home by noon.

Such technology usually epitomizes efficiency, but oddly, it has had to be designed to allow for inefficient routing—so that dispatchers can accommodate human needs. "Computers and mathematics don't care about human decision making," notes Tim Quinn, manager of GeoFields' transportation services,

The new ITN dispatch screen will replace a complicated manual system requiring spreadsheets and paper maps. It will also help make the ITN system easily replicable anywhere.

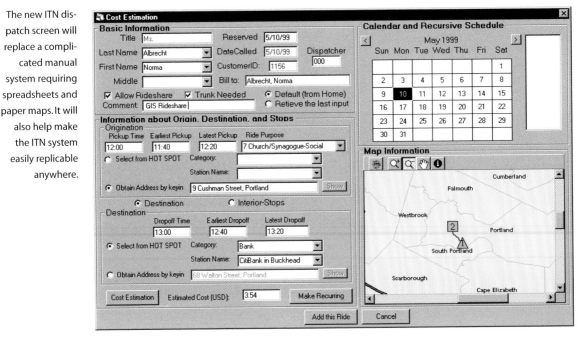

"because human decision making is very illogical." This design accommodates old friends who don't care if they have to go an extra, inefficient, 5 miles out of the way to have dinner at a favorite restaurant. Or, if two riders don't get along, as sometimes happens with human beings, the system lets the dispatcher keep them separated.

The system keeps track in the database of the financial accounts of each rider. Riders pay into their accounts, but others can too: their adult children, or local businesses looking for a way to give back to the community. Freund envisions a system in the future comprehensive enough so that elderly drivers could quit driving voluntarily, sell their cars, and put all the proceeds into their ITN account.

By most measures, the ITN model has been a success. In the Portland area, the number of rides ITN provided rose from 7,558 to 11,018, and the number of customers from 370 to 550, in just one year. The service has received national media coverage, and has expanded to a neighboring town.

The ITN system has caught the attention of policy makers in Maine, where the Speaker of the House of Representatives, G. Steven Rowe, has introduced a bill to spend $250,000 in state money, to be matched by private donations, to create an ITN program elsewhere in Maine. And Freund is exploring ways to expand the system nationally.

It may not be the toughest solution to the problem. But with the help of GIS, it will work.

*"Everyone has the right to life, liberty and security of person."*

Article III, Universal Declaration of Human Rights

# Chapter 6

# International

The global economy and the digital revolution have made the world interdependent as never before, and GIS is finding use across a broad spectrum of global needs. GIS allows common views of disparate lands, provides common tools for disparate tasks, and brings common understanding to disparate cultures.

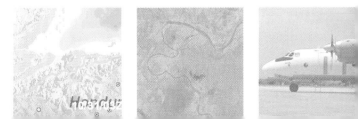

## You Cannot Fix What You Cannot See

IN OCTOBER 1998, Hurricane Mitch slammed into the east coast of Central America and lurched across the countryside for five days, smashing towns, burying thousands of people under mud flows, washing away neighborhoods and livelihoods, crushing life and hope. Every number associated with the damage was enormous: 180-mile-per-hour winds; 25 inches of rain in one six-hour period; 10,000 dead; and 6.5 million people hurt in some way. It was said to be the worst storm ever in the Western Hemisphere, and those who lived there were utterly unprepared for it.

"A panorama of death," the president of Honduras called the new landscape of his country.

The international relief community rushed to the area with equipment, supplies, and medical help, all the humanitarian resources and intentions customary for such disasters.

But you cannot fix what you cannot see.

Relief agencies and the region's governments needed information, and they

A relief map from the Digital Atlas of Central America shows the progress of Mitch across the landscape and the progress of destruction across Honduras.

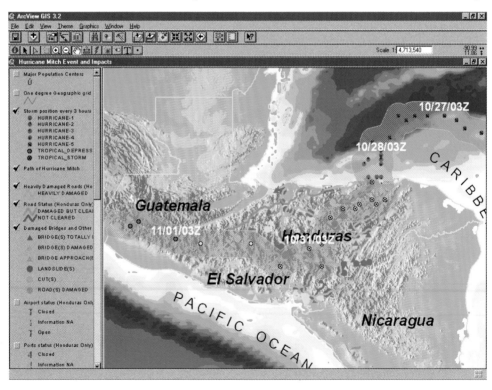

needed it fast: basic information about the Central American landscape and its roads, and even more importantly, information about which roads had been cut by landslides and floods, and where; which bridges were out and which towns isolated; who needed help the most and where they were.

But maps with the kind of accuracy and detail essential for search, rescue, and reconstruction—the kind of detailed maps that Americans take for granted—are hard to come by in this region. They were even harder to find after Mitch, and anyway, the physical

reality they reflected had been altered, perhaps forever.

Within days, GIS technology began to give the international community a clear picture of what had happened and where help was needed. Within weeks, those undertaking the reconstruction of this devastated land had several gigabytes of digital maps, aerial and satellite photos, and other information with which to begin that labor. And within months, with GIS providing policy makers a clear view of the devastation, Congress allocated funds that will see the development of a

Mitch's immense size dwarfed the countries of Central America as it smashed into the coastline, in this satellite view from the Digital Atlas.

comprehensive GIS network throughout Central America.

In many ways, the experience with Mitch showed GIS at its best.

One of the many calls for help that went out after Mitch struck was from national mapping agency officials in Honduras, who contacted their counterparts at the United States Geological Survey to say the storm had rendered them helpless. "All of their historical files, their aerial photography was gone," says James Jancaitis of the USGS, who directed and coordinated the GIS work in the following months. "Their ability to do their own disaster relief and planning was severely compromised." The USGS' boss, Interior Secretary Bruce Babbitt, then received a formal request for help from the Honduran government and Babbitt told USGS to do whatever needed to be done to help.

It was decided that the best way to help would be to find and consolidate all the available geographic information about the four affected countries (Honduras, Guatemala, El Salvador, and Nicaragua), put it into a common package and format that everyone could understand, and then distribute it to as many people as possible, as quickly as possible. A GIS was perfect for such a task.

A GIS can store huge amounts of information about a particular location. Layers of digital information about a location are, in effect, placed on top of each other on a basemap, and a user chooses which information to view by, in effect, peeling off or laying down a layer at a time. By combining layers, relationships become obvious. There is virtually no limit to the kinds of information that can be put in those layers.

A team of GIS programmers and specialists from ESRI's Washington, D.C., and California offices joined geologists, biologists, and other experts at the USGS Center for the Integration of Natural Disaster Information (CINDI) research lab in Virginia to create a Digital Atlas of Central America. Among the agencies represented at CINDI over the next few weeks were the National Oceanographic and Atmospheric Administration (NOAA), the National Imagery and Mapping Agency (NIMA), the CIA, the U.S. Air Force, the U.S. Army Corps of Engineers, several software and hardware companies, and the Centro Internacional de Agricultura Tropical of Colombia.

"There was a tremendous sense of urgency," says Jancaitis; the devastation was so extensive that even as the assembled team began its work, people were still being rescued. Jancaitis, Acting Senior Program Advisor for Map Data Collection and Integration for the USGS, acted as a kind of traffic controller, tracking down data from all over the world, persuading those who had it to share it, and directing it to the programmers and technicians, all of whom worked long hours with little sleep.

Their work was cut out for them. Spatial information, the kind you see when you look at a map, doesn't come in neat packages. Diverse kinds of data—maps of streets, river systems, and cropland—had to be reformatted. Paper maps had to be scanned and then converted to usable digital form. Aerial reconnaissance photos and satellite photos, a tremendous number of them, had to be georeferenced— an exacting process in which features on the photo are matched to geographic locations on the ground, using ArcView Image Analysis software. The teams also had to contend with converting data into standard latitude/longitude format so it would be usable by the greatest number of people.

Adding to the workload was the fact that all this diverse data comes from diverse sources, from commercial vendors to military forces to government agencies, each with a different attitude about how much information it is willing to share. One overgeneralization is that the more accurate and detailed the information, the less people want to share it, and the more money they want to do so.

But diversity of data also meant a diversity of products to serve the needs of a variety of relief organizations. The team created many thematic maps, each focused on a particular feature: rainfall amounts, crop locations, economic life, flood zones, and more. Places where

The Digital Atlas showed a wealth of information about soils, agriculture, and where new landslide dangers might be located.

more flooding and mudslides were still a danger also were mapped. Other information was not in a spatial format at all—for example, impassable bridges and roads, or ports that could only be used by small boats. The team matched this information to the locations on the GIS maps they were building, and spent much effort in designing meaningful graphic symbols to convey reality to as many people as possible.

Still other maps conveyed more narrow kinds of information: one, based on satellite imagery, showed the health of vegetation before and after Mitch; still another was a satellite image of Central America at night, showing the number of lights visible before and after—giving graphic evidence of the mess that the regional power grid was in.

All of this took weeks to assemble, but by Thanksgiving a Web site had gone up, built on ESRI's ArcView Internet Map Server software. It was updated, sometimes

daily, as more data became available to the team. Those in the field in Central America needed only a working phone line or a satellite link to access it.

To help with longer-term reconstruction efforts, the team released the digital atlases on CD–ROM, the first in January, and the second, which contained more than a gigabyte of compressed data, software, and imagery, in late February 1999. Each version was self-contained: a copy of ArcView Data Publisher, a special version of ArcView GIS, was bundled with the CD, and the company gave away two thousand copies. With the aid of another ESRI product, ArcPress™, the team produced scores of large, detailed paper maps.

ESRI also sent one of its applications programmers, Lisa Fastnaught of the Washington, D.C., office, to Honduras. Fastnaught stayed in the devastated capital of Tegucigalpa for a month, living amidst sorrow and devastation while

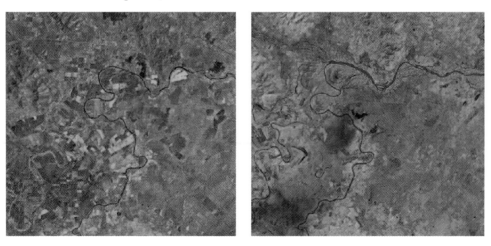

Before-and-after satellite imagery included on the Digital Atlas shows graphically how Hurricane Mitch affected the Rio Choluteca and changed its course.

creating digital maps and data specifically for that country, the hardest hit of all.

GIS was also used to show policy makers the extent of the damage so they could see for themselves why such a massive amount of help was needed.

Data, maps, and charts developed by the team at the CINDI lab were a key element of White House briefings on the disaster, which in turn led to President Clinton's establishment of a Central America reconstruction task force. The GIS materials were also used to compile a briefing book and atlas for Tipper Gore, who visited the country in mid-November, along with representatives Jim Kolbe of Arizona, Xavier Becerra of California, Gary Akerman of New York, and senators Christopher Dodd of Connecticut, Jeff Bingaman of New Mexico, and Mary Landrieu of Louisiana. Gore's briefing of President Clinton in turn led to a supplemental budget request for Central American relief that Congress finally approved in May.

ArcView GIS was a pivotal tool in helping get that legislation passed, says Jancaitis. He and Mark Schaefer, who was at the time the Interior Department's Acting Assistant Secretary for Water and Science, briefed many legislators and staffers on Capitol Hill. They used ArcView GIS on laptops to display the GIS maps of the devastation in graphic detail.

"Through the use of GIS we were able to rapidly show members of Congress and senior administration officials both the extent of damage caused by Hurricane Mitch and ways to respond to the needs of Central American countries," says Schaefer. "GIS was key to demonstrating how federal agencies, especially the USGS, can provide scientific and technical assistance to aid recovery and reconstruction activities. This was a key step in obtaining financial support for these efforts."

*In the years ahead I believe GIS w transform the way public policy decisio are made on many fronts, especially in the natural resources arena.*

**MARK SCHAEFER, FORMER ACTING ASSISTANT SECRETARY OF THE INTERIOR FOR WATER AND SCIENCE**

The use of GIS as a lobbying tool, to show policy makers an accurate graphic picture of reality, marks a notable maturation of the technology, in the view of both Jancaitis and Schaefer.

"In the years ahead I believe GIS will transform the way public policy decisions are made on many fronts, especially in the natural resources arena," Schaefer says.

With a supplemental appropriation of almost $1 billion, the USGS and other federal agencies have begun the next step in the disaster recovery. Paul Hearn, Bureau Coordinator of the USGS Hurricane Mitch Relief Program, put that next step this way: "You can't, in good conscience, help people recover from a disaster without helping them prepare for the next one."

Seventy municipalities in Honduras, Nicaragua, Guatemala, and El Salvador given the tools to build their own ...ehensive municipal GIS to help ...are for the next one. The towns will ...ve Internet access to larger regional ...ata facilities, and to humbler, more simple tools: stream gages, for example, will be linked to each town's GIS to give an early warning of rising flood waters.

A significant portion of a Honduran city of 120,000 called Choluteca was wiped out by Mitch because it was built on a floodplain. With a GIS in place, and with government officials trained in its capabilities, they can plan and avoid such mistakes when rebuilding the town. Choluteca has already begun that process: a stream gage is already in place.

"Now," says Hearn, "they can see what's coming."

map from ...igital Atlas ...bines a topo- ...aphic basemap with an aerial photo to show the extent of flooding and damage in the village of Choluteca, which will be one of the first areas to benefit from a new regional GIS infrastructure.

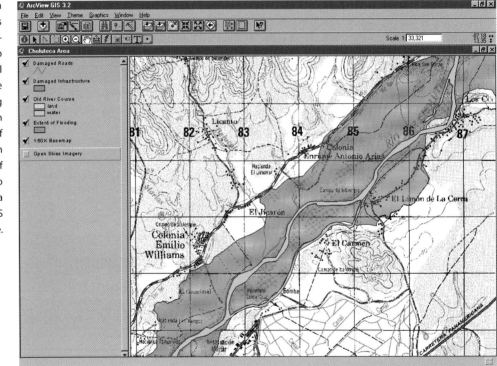

## After War, Mapping Peace

GEOGRAPHY is an inextricable part of war, but the technology of geography, GIS, has become an inextricable part of the struggle for peace—perhaps the oldest and most universal of public policies.

In the Balkans, site of some of the last large-scale warfare of the 20th century, GIS has been indispensable in treaty negotiations, in the reconstruction of a brutalized city, and in the delivery of relief supplies to refugees.

The geography of the Balkans was one of several critical considerations when Muslim, Croatian, and Serbian leaders met at Wright–Patterson Air Force Base in November 1995 to negotiate an end to hostilities that had killed 250,000 and brought a chilling new euphemism into the language: "ethnic cleansing."

There was a tentative agreement before the parties arrived in Ohio that Bosnia would be partitioned, with Muslims and Croats given authority over 51 percent of the territory, and 49 percent given to the Serbs. The precise boundaries of these two territories were to be settled and mapped at the talks.

Robert Aldridge of the Camber Corp., an Alabama software engineering firm, led a small team of ArcInfo specialists into the negotiations 10 days after they had begun. They joined other ArcInfo technicians from the U.S. Army Topographic Engineering Center, and instructors from the Defense Mapping Agency (later consolidated into the National Imagery and Mapping Agency), which had overall responsibility. The team set about streamlining and standardizing the mapping operation, organizing the dozens of proposals for partition boundaries floating around into one common file structure in ArcInfo.

The exact 51-percent/49-percent apportionment of territory had to be retained in any mapmaking that was done, since that was the basis on which the parties had agreed to talk in the first place. Calculating these percentages in each new boundary proposal throughout the negotiations was the ArcInfo team's primary task. Every day, negotiators for the three sides would haggle over the boundaries on paper U.N. road maps of 1:600,000 scale, drawing and erasing lines on them. The paper maps with their revised boundaries scrawled on them would be taken to the ArcInfo team to be digitized, and then transferred to more detailed, 1:50,000-scale topographic maps. The team would then calculate the percentage change in land area that had occurred with the redrawn boundaries. Then the whole process would begin over again. Using ArcInfo cut the time necessary to calculate these percentages in half, Aldridge says. Negotiators were also arguing over the size of buffer zones around the boundary line, and the software made the generation of these much easier.

To create another important tool for the negotiations, ArcInfo was combined with a 3-D visualization software package called Power Scene®, from Cambridge

State Department
geographers
David Smith and
William Wood cre-
ated these maps
in ArcView GIS to
show the move-
ment of ethnic
groups during
the Bosnian
civil war.

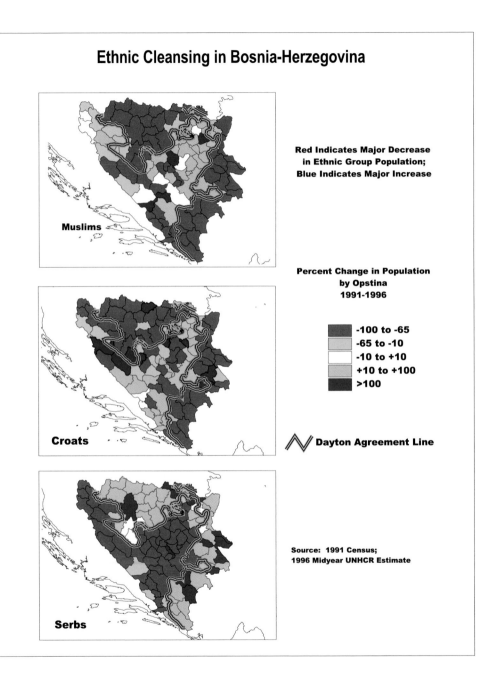

# Ethnic Cleansing in Bosnia-Herzegovina

**Muslims**

**Red Indicates Major Decrease
in Ethnic Group Population;
Blue Indicates Major Increase**

**Croats**

**Percent Change in Population
by Opstina
1991-1996**

-100 to -65
-65 to -10
-10 to +10
+10 to +100
>100

**Dayton Agreement Line**

**Serbs**

**Source: 1991 Census;
1996 Midyear UNHCR Estimate**

Research Associates. After digitizing new boundaries, the ArcInfo team would translate the geographic coordinates of the new line into an ASCII file for the Power Scene software. Using high-resolution aerial imagery, Power Scene would take negotiators on a virtual 3-D flyby up and down the new boundary line, through mountain passes and river valleys, so that they could see exactly what the territory they had just given to one side or the other looked like. This usually led to more tweaking of the boundary line, if only by a few hundred feet.

These simulations led to one breakthrough, an agreement on the size of a corridor that would link the city of Goradze with the rest of the Bosnian–Croat territory. Serbian president Slobodan Milosevic had insisted that the corridor to be carved through Serb territory could be no wider than 2 kilometers. Technicians gave Milosevic a virtual flyby down the corridor in question to show him that 2 kilometers was too narrow to be realistic. Milosevic backed down and allowed the corridor to be made wider.

The signing of a peace deal in Paris the following month meant not only an end to civil war, but also an end to the siege of Sarajevo, where residents had been enduring something close to hell on earth for three and a half years. The infrastructure of the city and suburbs was shattered, and utilities destroyed, says Azer Kurtovic, who heads up the Sarajevo office of GISDATA. The

company is an ESRI Business Partner and supplies data, maps, and training throughout the Balkans. Among GISDATA's clients using ESRI software are SarajevoGAS, Sarajevo's transportation and planning departments, and Bosnia's state electric utility, JPElektroprivreda BiH.

Another is the Zavod za planiranje razvoja Kanton Sarajevo, the urban planning institute of the Sarajevo region, which is helping plan how Sarajevo will be permanently rebuilt, with the aid of training and software grants from ESRI and from GISDATA.

The destruction of Sarajevo has also created opportunity, in the view of Lutfi Kapidzic, database manager of the institute's GIS department. Since the city must be rebuilt, it can be done according to principles of good urban design and landscape architecture. "It opens up a new frontier, new directions to find better solutions for some areas," Kapidzic says.

An alliance of professional and academic planners and students from around the world known as the Global Network for Rebuilding has formed to pool expertise and design ideas for the new Sarajevo. Founded by Jay Craig, an urban designer and landscape architect from Birmingham, Alabama, the organization, with very little money, has put together GIS training sessions and design studios, and has solicited design ideas from students, as part of its mission to rebuild cities devastated by war.

In the view of Craig, Kapidzic, and others involved in this work, the physical design of a new Sarajevo could even help heal the wounds of war. The city was previously a multiethnic, sophisticated place where residents prided themselves on incorporating cultural and ethnic differences to create a richer whole. However the war may have exploited ethnic or religious divisions, imaginative urban

and landscape planning could help bridge those divisions by creating spaces in the city to bring people together instead of separating them.

GIS has also been used in the Balkans for a different kind of postwar rebuilding effort, that of obtaining international justice. Because one of the techniques of

Negotiators at the Dayton peace talks in 1995 depended on maps like this, created with the help of ESRI's ArcInfo software, to delineate the exact boundary lines and buffer zones between the Federation of Bosnia and Herzegovina, and the Republika Srpska, the two political entities created in the aftermath of the Bosnian war of 1992 to 1995.

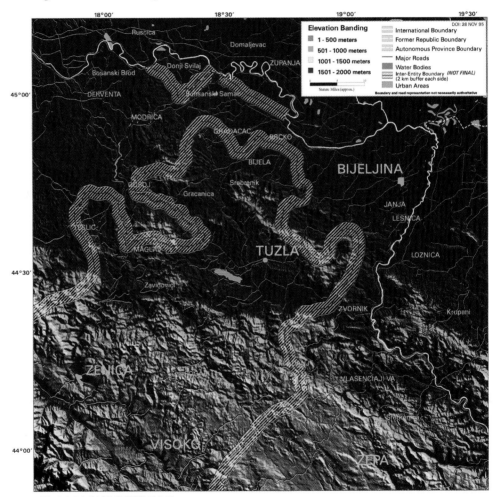

"ethnic cleansing" is mass expulsions of a people from a particular geographic area, it is also an activity that can be mapped in a GIS. And because a GIS can link a map to databases of relevant information, that means it could be used to link the war crimes in an area to the military and political force dominant there at the time. This is what State Department geographers David Smith and William Wood did with ArcView GIS.

They used a variety of data, including ArcInfo coverages of administrative areas known as *opstinas*, distributions of ethnic groups according to the most recent Yugoslavian census, U.N. estimates, and lists of missing persons from the International Committee of the Red Cross. From other international organizations, they obtained lists of mosques and other religious buildings that were known to have been destroyed. Much of this information needed additional work before it could be entered into the database. For example, place names often had different spellings that had to be

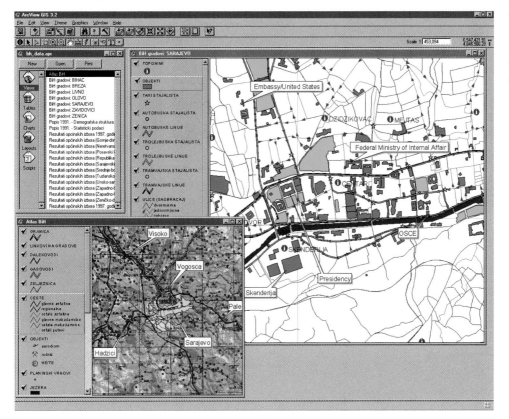

City and regional maps of Sarajevo by GISDATA created with ArcView GIS.

*Sometimes half a meter can save somebody's life.*

**MUHAMED MUMINOVIC, PROGRAM MANAGER, AMPHIBIA**

reconciled, and their exact latitude and longitude had to be calculated and entered into the database.

But once those tasks were done, the wholesale displacement of the Muslim population from certain areas of Bosnia, and their replacement by Serbs, was clearly evident; missing-person reports were concentrated in particular areas, as were reports of religious sites destroyed; reports of war crimes were clearly linked to those who had control of the region at the time.

Another rebuilding task in the Balkans is simply to make the land safe to walk on again: ArcView GIS is being used to clear landmines. The Sarajevo firm AMPHIBIA, under contract to the United Nation's Mine Action Centre, uses ArcView GIS to map the size and location of minefields in and around Sarajevo and other areas. Muhamed Muminovic, the firm's program manager, says the software allows the company to map the size of minefields, the areas that have been cleared and not cleared, and the exact geographic coordinates of the field, down to the meter. This kind of precision is key to his operation: "Sometimes half a meter can save somebody's life," he says. It is a job that will keep AMPHIBIA and other companies busy

for years; there are thousands of mines scattered around the Balkan landscape.

Three years after the signing of the Bosnia peace in Paris, war broke out again in the Balkans, this time to the south, over the future of the Serbian province of Kosovo. NATO began an air campaign against Serbia, and thousands of Kosovars fled their villages, holing up in the countryside, seeking refuge from war, with little more than the clothes on their backs. Some were said to be subsisting on leaves and tree bark.

The venerable International Rescue Committee launched a mission to send food and other supplies to them, a mission underwritten by the Agency for International Development's Office of U.S. Foreign Disaster Assistance (USAID/ OFDA). The committee hired Toronto-based Skylink Aviation to fly the missions, and they in turn chartered two aging Russian-built Antonov 26b cargo planes to make the drops. It was a dangerous assignment. NATO said it could not guarantee the safety of the planes and pilots, and the Serb government called the missions "unacceptable," and said the planes might be shot down.

The flights, from the Italian city of Pescara across the Adriatic Sea into Kosovo and back again, therefore had to be flown precisely: the flight corridors were narrow and the pilots could fly them only very early in the morning, before NATO flights resumed and the air would again be filled with projectiles. Moreover, the planes had to fly high over the drop areas, about 13,000 feet, to avoid small arms fire from the ground. The pilots had to account for wind speed and direction at that height, in order to drop the specially packaged supplies and food without parachutes.

Conventional paper aviation charts of the area were inadequate for the job. So

the flight team on the ground included a cartographer, Nate Smith of the Office of Foreign Disaster Assistance. Using ArcView GIS and ArcView Spatial Analyst and data from the National Imagery and Mapping Agency (NIMA) and from NATO, Smith created customized maps for the pilots, assisted by Simon Cottingham of ESRI's distributor in the United Kingdom.

ArcView GIS and ArcView Spatial Analyst allowed Smith and Cottingham to make maps that were specifically and precisely designed for each flight, and to

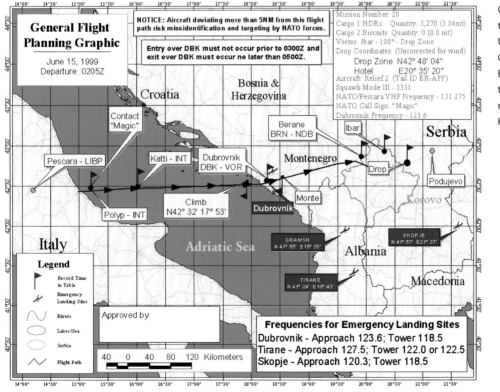

One of the maps that Nate Smith of USAID and Simon Cottingham of ESRI (UK) Ltd. put together for the relief flights into Kosovo.

include just the information needed; conventional flight maps contained a great deal of extraneous information that could confuse the Moldovan pilots, who spoke little English. GIS technology also allowed more flexibility. Conditions changed, sometimes each day, during the month-long operation: the drop zone coordinates would be moved, or the flight path across the Adriatic might be changed a few miles this way or that, depending on NATO's battle plans. They were able to use the layout abilities of ArcView GIS to simplify mapmaking, making it easier and faster to change only those conditions on the maps that needed to be changed. In order to give pilots the latest information, the maps were created at 2 A.M. for a departure two hours later.

The pilots were at first suspicious of the newfangled printouts, says Cottingham, being used to conventional aviation charts. But once they saw how each map could be customized for each flight and how accurate they were, the resistance disappeared. The maps also served as a way to bridge the language barrier between flight planners and pilots.

In the hands of those trying to bring peace out of war, GIS can be a most powerful weapon.

One of the Russian-built cargo planes used to drop relief supplies.

## Internet Resources

The GIS in Public Policy Web site, at *www.esri.com/esripress/publicpolicy*, provides an Internet gateway for readers wanting to know more about how GIS is helping answer questions of public policy —or, to paraphrase former California Governor Jerry Brown—helping to pose the right questions about public policy.

At this Web site, readers will find links to the organizations profiled in the book, links to those doing similar work, and links to related organizations.

Also available at the site are links to full-text papers on GIS and public policy issues, given at the annual ESRI International User Conference in recent years. These papers are available through the library at the ESRI Virtual Campus (*campus.esri.com*), which offers training and instruction in GIScience, technology, and applications. From the Virtual Campus Library, readers can further access thousands of papers, abstracts, and publications not only from ESRI's conferences but also from other public-policy-related organizations, such as the Urban and Regional Information Systems Association (URISA).

Bookmark *www.esri.com/esripress/ publicpolicy* and check back often for new developments and resources.

*R. W. Greene*
*rwgreene@esri.com*